D1725541

STARK NAKED NUMBERS

UNCOVER YOUR FINANCIALS, UNLOCK YOUR CASH, AND UNLEASH YOUR PROFITS

JASON ANDREW

arbor
GROUP

Published by the Arbor Group
4/155 Queen Street, Brisbane, QLD 4000, Australia

Andrew, Jason.
Stark naked numbers : uncover your financials, unlock your cash, and unleash your profits.
ISBN 978-0-6484240-0-0

Printed in the United States of America
Set in Minion
Designed by Fredrick Haugen

To Liz
You are the Dr to my Cr.

CONTENTS

Introduction: Time to Get Naked

We lie about what success looks like. Luckily, I found a better way.

Principle 1: Make Yourself Redundant

Rather than being stuck in your business, scale yourself from it.

Principle 2: Maximize Your Margins

Revenue is overrated. Margins are what really matters.

Principle 3: Super-Charge Your Cash Flow

Revenue is vanity. Profit is sanity. Cash is reality.

Principle 4: Leverage Your Assets

I'm not just talking about physical assets. People are assets as well.

Principle 5: Sharpen The Saw

Achieving any goal is based on good habits that you practice daily.

Conclusion: Naked as a Way of Life

Learn to see your numbers stark naked.

Introduction

TIME TO GET NAKED

NUMBERS REVEAL THE TRUTH

Like many business owners, I lied to myself about what
success looked like. I hid behind my financials and (even worse)
ignored them. But no more. I found a better way.

"We suffer more often in imagination than in reality."

Seneca

UNDRESS YOURSELF

Hiding From Reality in My Bed

I hit snooze on my alarm for the eleventeenth time that Wednesday afternoon. "Just one more hour," I repeated to myself. I tossed and turned in my bed sheets, struggling to contain the restlessness and anxiety.

After much deliberation, I flung away the pillow I'd used to suffocate the light and noise of the outside world.

Squinting as the afternoon sun peeked through my bedroom curtain, I grabbed my phone and cleared the dozens of missed calls and emails piling up in my inbox.

"4 p.m. already?" I muttered to myself.

Everyone's day had already finished. Mine hadn't even started.

I wanted the anxiety to end. So I made a decision. Quitting my business, then and there, was the obvious remedy.

I reached for my journal and documented the steps.

- Fire our staff
- Refer our clients to another firm
- Wind up the company
- Get a real job
- Pay off my personal and business debt

One thing I enjoy is problem solving. And closing the company I founded three years earlier would be a relieving problem to solve. I rationalized the process in my mind.

Failure is okay, right? I can always make the money back. What about all the time spent during the last three years? Well, I'll just consider that a sunk cost. Perhaps I'm not cut out to be an entrepreneur. I should go back to a real job. At least I'll get paid a market salary, compared to the pittance I've been drawing for the last few years.

I'll be stuck with some debt, but I could pay that back over time.

It'll be easy to just quit.

At least I'll be happy.

A Moment of Clarity

I felt oddly content after journaling the steps to quit my business. Actually, I was proud of it. It was the best work I'd done all year.

Feeling better about the situation, it was time to get the day started. I dragged myself into the shower.

As hot water blasted down my back, I stared blankly at the porcelain tiles. No thought immediately came to mind, but seconds later, I couldn't help but explore the reasons to quit my business.

I reflected on the last six, especially difficult, months.

Here were the events at play:

- We had close to no cash in the bank
- We had next to no new sales for 4 consecutive months
- We churned 15% of our total revenue in 6 weeks
- We let go of 2 staff members
- We had committed to employing 3 new staff
- Our burn rate and losses were increasing
- We had no line of sight for accessing additional capital

It wasn't just the continuous series of disappointments, setbacks, and financial problems.

It was that I felt like an imposter. A fraud.

I spent my entire career working with business owners to help them manage their finances—helping them improve and navigate the challenges they faced in good times and bad. Yet, my own firm was on the verge of bankruptcy.

I was supposed to be the fiscally responsible accountant! The financial compass for my clients. But how could I run a business that advised other business owners on how to control their finances when I couldn't even handle my own?

Quitting was the right decision. Not just my company, but the accounting and finance profession altogether.

Undress Yourself

As I wiped away the fogged up bathroom mirror, a tired jaded face presented itself.

I spent a moment to stare blankly at my stark naked body. A reflection of myself at the lowest point in my entire career.

I was stark naked, exposed in my truest form.

For once in a long time, I had nothing to hide. This was it.

I looked hard at myself to understand what I truly wanted. I needed to get down to the truth. Whether that was good or bad, I needed to see things for what they really were.

The positive self-talk started playing in my head:

- *Billions of people are worse off than I. My life is amazing.*
- *I didn't work this hard just to give it all up.*
- *The alternative to working for someone else has greater risks than working for myself.*
- *This is just a small obstacle I need to overcome.*
- *I don't need to have the answers, I simply need to understand the problems better.*

Still naked, I ran into my bedroom and started journaling again. As I articulated the problems I was facing, I started to see things more clearly. The emotionally heavy, depressive fog was clouding my judgment, limiting my ability to think clearly.

Call it a moment of clarity or vulnerability, but I came to a place where I realized this was exactly what I needed to do for my company.

I needed to uncover my business to reveal the truth. To see my problems for what they really were, then fix them.

I got to work.

You Are The Story You Tell Yourself

Hindsight is a wonderful thing. Reflecting on that day that I hid in my bed, it's incredible how dramatic I imagined the situation to be.

The reality was that our business wasn't as bad as I thought. By all accounts, it was actually doing well. Indeed, we had some hiccups, but if I was to view our corporate journey as a marathon, that 6-month period was simply a speed bump at the third mile. I mean to say that our situation was really small-time stuff.

Hundreds of thousands of small business owners and startups go through these challenges each and every day—most of which are a hundred times worse than mine. The circumstances for my company were trivial. Although, at the time, it felt like the perfect storm. I was caught up in a spiral of negative self-talk—my version of imposter syndrome, the self-deprecating inner dialogue that becomes so real that we believe it to be true.

When we're caught in challenging situations—scenarios where there is no easy answer—we have a tendency to think and act irrationally. We use stories to fill in the gaps of information. We over-analyze things and create a narrative that is (quite often) not a reflection of reality.

Most of the time, these stories are completely ridiculous. However, in a heightened state of emotion, it's hard to see the situation in any other way.

Remember that time you assumed your wallet had been stolen because you couldn't find it? Or the time that branded placebo cured your splitting headache? These are examples of how we use stories to help us function. They're the brain's coping mechanisms to deal with challenging situations, to help us make fast decisions in times of discomfort and crisis.

This technique was useful when our homo-sapien ancestors dealt with real predatory threats, like saber-tooth tigers. But in the information age, it often fails us. I told myself that my entire business and career was a write-off. The truth was that I was simply overreacting.

I was lying to myself.

I'm a liar. And so are you.

"The intellect should be the servant of the heart, but not its slave."

Auguste Comte

NUMBERS DON'T LIE

Entrepreneurs Are Liars

Yep, you heard me correctly.

You, me, and every other founder and CEO trying to build a successful and profitable business… We're all liars.

When we're not having nervous breakdowns, we tell ourselves that everything is fantastic. We're solving the world's problems, having fun, and living in a constant state of purpose, drive, and ambition.

But, deep in our heart, we know that this is rarely the case.

Being a liar in this way is a good thing, even necessary. Because building a business is hard. And a little positivity goes a long way.

Even when things are going terribly wrong—like when there's not enough cash to meet next month's payroll—it's okay. We remain confident, and reassure ourselves that everything is going to be fine. We keep pushing forward. We rely on these stories to coach us through the good times, and the bad.

This type of positive outlook is often referred to as a 'reality distortion field'—a term made famous by Apple icon Steve Jobs.

As entrepreneurs, we operate in this distortion field every day. Think of your daily hustle: leaping out of bed every morning with a winner's mentality, ready to chew up and swallow whatever challenge is thrown at you. We all need a bit of that Jobs bravado.

The reality distortion field is great and it works—until it doesn't. It can work against us. We can get caught so deep in our own self-talk that we miss the details, the important clues. We begin to delude ourselves and assume that whatever we know must be true. It causes us to make decisions based on our personal biases and emotional whims; on 'gut feel'.

Then, there's a breaking point.

A key employee resigns. Our largest customer leaves to a competitor. The bank balance is on near empty. We kick into crisis mode, making 'executive decisions'.

We need to sell more! We need to call in our debtors! We need to cut payroll!

In this state of flux, our focus is on survival. We set aside the strategy, the vision, and the 20-page business plan presented to investors. Instead, we turn our attention to the present. We make short-term decisions to survive. Decisions that are often contrary to our vision and values.

Decisions that often cause us to fail.

I've been there. You've been there. It happens to all of us. It's part of what makes us human.

It's easy to get lost in the day-to-day grind of running a business. Operating in the trenches each day and night, we often don't have the time to step back and check on how things are really doing. To view things from afar, or what famed investor Ray Dalio refers to as 'higher level thinking'.

When we're caught in the grind, it's easy to make assumptions and estimates. And, when the reality distortion field is in full effect, those assumptions can be inaccurate and misleading. We naturally have an inflated sense of growth, or we underestimate the costs of running our business.

When those hunches go unchecked, so does our ability to make good decisions.

Numbers Tell a Story About the Truth

Numbers are the antidote. They are the source of truth that can poke holes in your reality distortion field. They're not influenced by your state of mind. They are binary and bring objective reality to our often emotionally-charged decision processes.

Numbers don't just ground us; they can help us take a step back and assess things with higher-level thinking. This lens provides us with a different perspective. A frame that enables us to make more rational decisions.

Your company's financial statements are a useful tool. They are a reflection of your performance, how things are really doing. They also leave clues—important clues on how to improve cash flow, to scale your business, what to do next.

Your financial statements tell a story. You just need to learn what they're trying to show you.

As a chartered accountant and entrepreneur, I've worked with hundreds of businesses—ranging from small businesses and startups—all the way to publicly-traded companies. I've stripped back the covers and shone a clarifying light into the darkness of their financials—helping them to understand the clues that are hidden in financial statements. My skill is teaching people how to see them. I love this craft so much that I built a business around doing it.

What I enjoy most about my calling is the art of deconstruction. When I review a set of financial statements, I assess them the same way a house flipper would size up a down-trodden 'fixer upper'. I see opportunity. Like stripping an old rotting house to its frame, it is satisfying to pick apart a business to its fundamental elements—identifying structural strengths and weaknesses, then suggesting remedies for improvement.

After reviewing hundreds of businesses through an analytical lens, I've begun to spot patterns. I've learned the rules that separate the superstar businesses from the average ones. The characteristics that divide the efficient, highly-profitable businesses (that seem to print cash) from the mediocre ones that struggle every month just to reach break-even.

I was surprised to learn that the differences between these businesses was not subject to the industry, size, or even the traits of the CEO or founder (although those factors are important). Rather, the indicators were attributable to the financial habits of the company itself.

I discovered that it's disciplined attention to the numbers that propels a company to lasting greatness. The most successful firms quantify everything and observe what the numbers are saying. Business, after all, is a numbers game.

Accounting is Failing You

You started your business, I suspect, for two reasons. One: to do something you love. To build a legacy. To solve big, interesting problems and leave your mark on the world. And two: for financial freedom. You started it to generate some degree of wealth.

Whatever your reason, there is a direct correlation to knowing your numbers and your chance of success. As Warren Buffett says, "Accounting is the language of business". And, if you can't speak the language, how do you know where you are heading?

So why don't we pay more attention to numbers?

Well, firstly, we're not all accountants. A large corporation has the resources to employ teams of experts, financial analysts, and a CFO to focus strict attention to the numbers. Cash, in this case, is a competitive advantage.

So where does that leave you, the entrepreneur that doesn't have the resources to splurge on financial firepower? How do you make good financial decisions like the big guys?

Well, you could always learn about accounting yourself. Right? You know, go to the library or find some Investopedia articles online where you can learn about Luca Pacioli and the invention of double-entry bookkeeping. Fun stuff, like why debits must always equal credits.

Or, you could ask your CPA for tax advice. Remember Bob? The guy that seems to be more concerned about the tax deductibility of your entertainment bill, rather than the fact that you've incurred losses for the last three quarters.

Let's face it: accounting is boring. The concepts are dressed up with corporate jargon and confusing acronyms like EBITDA, FCF, and ROCE. Alphabet soup. It's a domain closely guarded by academics who've spent decades rewriting university textbooks for ever-changing accounting standards. The profession is complete with practitioners that don't understand how business works. They're incentivized to speak in tongues in order to guard their hourly billing rates.

You know what makes it even more difficult? Accounting can be misleading. That's right. The numbers on your Balance Sheet and your Profit & Loss aren't reflective of your actual financial position. At best, they're a crude approximation.

Furthermore, traditional financial statements were not designed to help you make decisions in the trenches. They are dressed up, invented by academics to stop billion-dollar corporations from deceiving investors and shareholders with 'creative accounting'—a sinister sleight-of-hand that has resulted in the collapse of firms like Enron, the one-time Wall Street darling.

The story of Enron is similar to Hans Christian Andersen's fairy tale, *The Emperor's New Clothes*. Remember that one? It's about a narcissistic emperor who cared nothing about the truth of his situation. His only concern in life was looking good and bragging about that to the world. Except, with Enron, it wasn't fiction.

Noted investor Warren Buffett knows all the tricks adopted by companies to manipulate financial statements. His fund, Berkshire Hathaway, employs teams of analysts to pour over the statements of potential investments—making funky adjustments to uncover the financials, just to understand the true financial performance of a business, to eliminate the noise and understand what's real.

Accounting fails entrepreneurs every single day. It's failing you.

Uncover Your Financials

I developed my 'accounting chops' from years of helping my clients. But it wasn't until I started my own business that I understood how to use numbers to drive decision-making.

Working with entrepreneurs, I've found that the primary reason why accounting is so confusing is none of us was ever taught functional literacy with numbers. Most content out there is pregnant with academic concepts and jargon that are largely irrelevant to your business. There's no practical guide to help you understand, plain and simple, what's important to your success.

The truth is that accounting is not difficult subject matter. Despite the stereotype, you don't need to be good at algebra or statistics. Despite what your accountant says, you don't need to know the difference between a debit and a credit.

All you need to know are fundamental principles: the raw, naked numbers that are meaningful to your company's growth.

Being both an accountant and entrepreneur myself, I wrote this book to help entrepreneurs, like you—to make your numbers work.

This book is about leverage, how to hack your accounting for success. Applying Pareto's Principle, I'll teach you the core financial principles that will maximize your financial return with the absolute minimum effort. Simply put, you'll learn which 20% of your numbers actually create 80% of the measurable impact.

This book is complete with actionable, practical insights into how you can improve and grow your business. I'm going to share with you techniques that can improve your cash flow, grow profitability, scale your business, and even predict the future.

No jargon, no stuffiness, no bullshit. Just stripped back, useful tools, methods, and insights used by the very best companies that you can implement in your very own business—irrespective of your size, industry, or geography.

The numbers matter. Your financial statements tell a story. Let me help you uncover what they're trying to show you, and how you can use them to your advantage.

"Who's it for?"

Seth Godin

WHO'S YOUR CUSTOMER?

Context is Everything

We all know that your financials only tell one part of a story. A Profit & Loss statement doesn't say anything about who you serve and what you sell. Context, therefore is everything.

To provide context around the numbers, it's important to understand the type of business you're in. The traditional way to do this is to separate companies into those that manufacture and build physical products, and those that provide some type of service. You may have encountered this concept in a myriad of accounting and entrepreneurship courses, seminars, and books.

I've got a different way of thinking about your company, one that's in line with how business is done today.

What's much more important is how you interact with your customer, not what product or service you offer. I like to call it a distinction between 'high-touch' and 'low-touch'.

High-Touch and Low-Touch Business Models

Ask yourself this question: What does a professional services firm like PricewaterhouseCoopers (PwC) have in common at all with an automotive distributor like the Penske Corporation?

At first glance, you might say—besides being global brands—not much. In fact, you could argue that these businesses don't have many similarities. They operate in different industries, sell different types of products, even operate in different markets.

I actually think they have a lot in common.

Penske and PwC share traits in their business model. They're both heavily reliant on people. They primarily work in B2B. But mostly, they are high-touch businesses. By high-touch, I mean that the nature of the product and services they sell are time intensive. Their clients have high expectations and risk is often greater as well. The average deal size is also relatively high, which typically comes with long sales cycles. Because of this, they can more easily price their product and service on value, as opposed to just cost.

What are the similarities between an e-commerce company like Harry's and a software-as-a-service (SaaS) business like Basecamp? Both their offerings are financially accessible to a large market. The engagement process to purchase from them is automated and often requires little to no human interaction.

These attributes make their value propositions highly scalable, with the ability to quickly reach a global customer base. In addition, both are subscription-based—meaning an ongoing annuity and cash flow stream.

You see, beneath the veil of industry type and brand, there are an array of businesses that can be categorized into two types of business models. They may be completely different from the outside, however—from a financial perspective—their challenges are largely the same.

In order to illustrate the various financial tactics that high-touch and low-touch businesses can take, we'll discuss two case studies: the ficticious companies Voltage Media and Moo Formula. We'll follow them throughout the book—looking at their key challenges and how they use financial analysis to provide valuable insights and to diagnose problems. Let's meet each of the founders.

First up, Brendan.

Voltage Media

"Do you think I'm insane?"

Brendan asked this as he polished off his seventh pint of beer for the evening (what I was hoping would be the last round). I'd gotten to the bar earlier that night and settled down with a vodka soda, knowing full well that Brendan would be running late as usual. After 30 minutes he showed up—wearing his signature blue skinny jeans and black t-shirt.

Brendan stands six-foot-two, broad shoulders, and a frame any footballer would envy. I watch him as he eagerly strolls through the entrance, pacing around the bar for a few seconds until we make eye contact. He runs over and greets me, offering a generous grin— white pearly teeth contrasted against his thick beard.

I could picture Brendan leveraging his natural charm and charisma in the boardrooms of his corporate clients. It must be the secret sauce for his firm Voltage Media LLC—a digital marketing consultancy that has grown to 15 employees in less 2 years.

Brendan was a salaryman for his entire career. That was until he was laid off when his employer went belly up. It was the third time he'd been made redundant due to problems out of his control. He decided it was time to take charge of his own destiny.

After settling in with small talk and the first round of drinks, I jump right to it.

"So, how's business?" I ask.

It's not until he glares at me do I see the bags formed under his bloodshot eyes, caused by what looks like sleep deprivation rather than booze.

"Well, where do I start?" he says. "We just landed five new consulting clients, all five-figure engagements."

"That's great news!" I say.

"Yes, well it is," he retorts. "But the problem is my team are already doing crazy hours. I can't keep up with workload and I don't have the cash to hire more staff. I'd do it myself, but I'm already managing my share of clients. These 90-hour weeks are taking a toll. My wife is sick of me working weekends and I haven't seen my kids in over a month."

"I agree, that is a problem," I say, "but a good one to have."

"Glad you think about it that way," he responds, "but I feel like I'm getting screwed financially as well. I am barely drawing enough of a salary to cover my mortgage and living expenses. I've got mouths to feed, man!"

He continues, "I knew this business was going to be hard, and I was prepared to put in the work, but I don't feel like I'm paying myself enough. For the amount of hours I'm doing, I'm better off working at McDonalds!"

"Let's see what the numbers numbers are telling us," I say.

Brendan yanks a laptop from his leather satchel, while I grab an unused napkin from the counter—and we get to work.

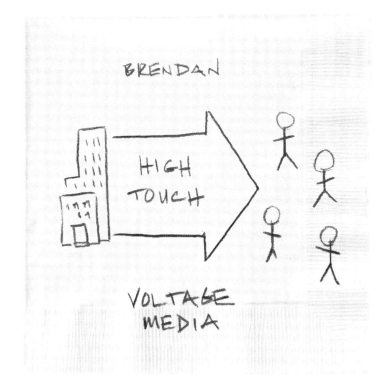

The evening wound down with a less-heated conversation about the future and vision for his company. We spoke about what little tweaks we could make to improve his cash flow, and how this tied into the bigger picture. The edge was taken off, assured that a plan was in place.

Three and a half hours after we started, Brendan closed his laptop, made a move to get up and then paused.

"Do you think I'm insane?" he asked.

I glanced away, trying my best to garner a witty response—but simply shrugged. A split second second later, we shook hands and Brendan drove off in his Tesla.

BRENDAN'S KEY FINANCIAL CHALLENGES

- When can I afford to hire my next employee?
- How can I increase my profit?
- Where is my cash?
- When can I afford to pay myself a higher salary?
- How do I improve my cash flow?
- How do I calculate my charge-out rate?
- What numbers should I looking at?

Moo Formula

"I just cannot stand incompetence!"

On first impression, Sarah appears to be a cold business woman. She's bold, abrupt, and carries a posture of pure discipline. To an outsider, she's an intimidating character. But it's a front.

Beneath this veil, she is a generous and compassionate person just like the rest of us. I imagine you'd have to maintain a stoic front as a mother of two, and the co-founder/CEO of Moo Formula Inc., a venture-backed e-commerce startup.

We are sitting in the boardroom of the newly fitted-out office when she shares with me the financial results for the last quarter.

"I'm satisfied with the operations," she says, "but I feel like we're burning through our cash flow too quickly without growth. We've missed our revenue budget for the last four consecutive months and the Board is getting concerned."

She continues, "We've got six months of runway left, and if we don't fix it, we'll have to take another round of investment which I don't want to do. We've already diluted enough."

I first met Sarah at a Shopify meet-up. She was perched at the front of the audience in a red dress and matching handbag. She was one of those naturally curious people, questioning everything. She's willing to ask the 'dumb' questions that everyone else is afraid to do. Her confidence and ability to think critically are her greatest assets.

We bumped into each other at the drinks cart where she shared her journey of raising financing for her first venture.

Moo Formula is a subscription-based organic baby formula business. The company sources raw ingredients, manufactures them, and sells tubs of organic baby formula direct to consumers.

Sarah founded the company with her husband and business partner, Mark, after her challenges finding quality, trusted brands of baby formula for her two young children.

"As a marketing executive and mother of two, I struggled to keep up with the day-to-day grind of running errands," she said.

After three consecutive years of triple-digit revenue growth, the company raised its first round of venture capital funding just six months ago. While sales were growing, they were short of the projections. Furthermore, the company's suppliers jacked up their prices knowing how well the business was doing.

Back in the boardroom, Sarah looks at me, "I think the problem is that we're spending too much to acquire our customers."

"What makes you think that?" I ask.

"Well, we keep pumping more and more money into Facebook campaigns, but our sales are not growing like they used to."

I review the financial report and run a quick analysis of the key metrics on the back of a napkin.

Sarah's intuition was right—the company had a customer churn problem. Not only that, they had a problem with their gross profit margins as a result of the supplier price increases.

SARAH'S KEY FINANCIAL CHALLENGES

- How much can I spend on customer acquisition?
- How can I increase my profit?
- How do I calculate my burn rate and runway?
- What reports do my investors want to see?
- How do I calculate my break-even point?
- How do I improve my gross profit?
- How can I increase my revenue?

The Tale of Two Entrepreneurs

A high-touch business can be described as one that involves a high level of personal, human interaction. They involve larger deal sizes and commonly have a longer business sales cycle.

Low-touch business, on the other hand, can be described as having a lower package size, and is more scalable in its distribution to customers. These customers may have a high level of brand loyalty, however they are price conscious.

Brendan of Voltage Media is a great example of a high-touch business model. Conversely, Sarah's business Moo Formula is an example of a low-touch business model.

Throughout this book, both Brendan's and Sarah's businesses will be used as case studies to break down and apply the various financial tactics, methodologies, and principles applicable to both high-touch and low-touch business models.

Here's a summary of the type of industries in each model:

HIGH-TOUCH BUSINESS MODEL

- Professional Services
- Hospitality
- Trades and other services
- Wholesale/Manufacturing

LOW-TOUCH BUSINESS MODEL

- Retail
- E-Commerce
- Software as a Service (SaaS)
- Marketplace

Every business is unique, but many of the financial challenges they face are not. The tools and tactics in this book cover the most common money problems experienced in business. Although the challenges will be the same, remedies and tactics will slightly differ, dependent on the high-touch or low-touch model.

The Munger Advantage: Mental Models

Charlie Munger, right-hand adviser to Warren Buffett, is regarded as one of the world finest thinkers. The two business partners have worked together for nearly 60 years, investing wisely to make Berkshire Hathaway the multi-billion dollar firm it is today.

Individually, Munger is known for his unparalleled ability to make intelligent, long-term, rational decisions. His near perfect track record of picking investments that outperform the market is a claim to that. What does he do differently to the rest of us?

The answer is a set of mental models—a latticework of principles he has developed himself—drawn from a variety of disciplines, from physics to biology.

Munger is acutely aware of all the cognitive flaws that humans possess. His defense is a set of principles to aid him in critical decisions. In a famous talk at USC Business school in 1994, Munger explained his approach to attaining practical wisdom:

> *"You've got to hang experience on a latticework of models in your head. What are the models? The first rule is that you've got to have multiple models because if you just have one or two that you're using, the nature of human psychology is such that you'll torture reality so that it fits your models. And the models have to come from multiple disciplines because all the wisdom of the world is not to be found in one little academic department."*

The recommendations in this book don't contain the antiquated theory found in your Accounting 101 university textbook. This is the new, practical way of looking at your numbers. It's written for 21st Century business people, like you and me.

How To Use This Book

Applying Munger's concept as our starting point, I have distilled the variety of financial tools and tactics into a set of financial principles that you can build into your own mental model. These concepts are a framework you can lean on to make financial decisions like the best in business.

The 5 Principles are:

1. MAKE YOURSELF REDUNDANT

You are not your business. Rather than being stuck in it, your objective is to scale yourself from it. This section explores how to better use your financials so your business isn't dependent on you.

2. MANAGE YOUR MARGINS

Revenue is overrated. Margins are what really matters. In this section, we focus on the key profit metrics that you need to check the pulse on—and offer tactical approaches to improve them.

3. OPTIMIZE YOUR CASH FLOW

Revenue is bullshit. Sorry, let me say that more gently. I think revenue is vanity. Profit is sanity. Cash is reality. In this section, you'll learn how to convert your business into a cash flow machine.

4. LEVERAGE YOUR ASSETS

To create a valuable business, you must build assets and leverage them. And I'm not just talking about physical assets. Hint: People are assets, too.

5. SHARPEN THE SAW

Acheiving any goal is the accumulation of good habits that you practice daily. In this section, we explore a recipe book of metrics to help you transform your business into a well-oiled machine.

Choose Your Own Adventure

Although reading this book from start to finish is the suggested course of action, I've designed it for you to skip through—pick and choose the topics and tactics most relevant to your business.

Business challenges are fluid. They evolve and change. My goal is that you can use this as a handbook, a practical guide to help you deal with whatever financial hurdle you face.

I've included a number of blank napkins throughout the book. Use them to do your own calculations.

Go ahead and scribble away, take notes, and spill coffee on it. My goal is for the pages to be graffitied with your ink and, in the end, be your own rough sketch toward financial mastery.

Let's begin.

Principle 1

MAKE YOURSELF REDUNDANT

YOU ARE NOT YOUR BUSINESS

Rather than being stuck in it, your objective is to scale yourself from it. This section explores how to better use your financials so your business isn't dependent on you.

"*It's not about creating an object. It is about creating a perspective.*"

Albert Paley

YOUR BUSINESS IS A MACHINE

The Cashflow Quadrant

I had an interest in money from an early age—mainly because, when I was growing up, we didn't have much of it.

One of the first books about personal finance that I ever read was *Rich Dad's Cashflow Quadrant: Guide to Financial Freedom* by Robert Kiyosaki. The book has something of a cult following. In it, Kiyosaki frames four approaches to building wealth. Yet only two can help you to break free of the day-to-day grind. He explains that each of us falls into one of the following quadrants:

EMPLOYEE – THE E QUADRANT

Your income is derived via a salary which you cannot control. No matter how hard you work, your income will always be capped.

SELF-EMPLOYED – THE S QUADRANT

This describes the majority of people who call themselves 'business owners'—even those with a number of employees. In this quadrant, the company is entirely dependent on the owner's time.

If he or she stops working, their income stops as well.

BUSINESS OWNER – THE B QUADRANT

This is the realm of entrepreneurs, people who design systems—machines comprised of people and processes to generate a profit.

INVESTOR – THE I QUADRANT

Investors use money to create more money. They don't have to work because their money is working for them.

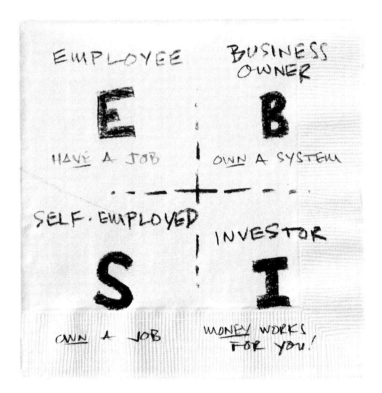

Are You an S or a B?

Unless one is a child prodigy entrepreneur, all of us started in the E Quadrant; we were employees once upon a time. Then we created a business. And bought into a misconception. We thought we were headed straight to being a Business Owner (the B Quadrant).

But what typically happens is that we shift from Employee to Self-Employed. Rather than owning a business, we own a job.

Let that sink in.

And I'm not just talking about solopreneurs here—the freelance designer working from a home office. You can be in the S Quadrant and have a dozen employees in a fancy office space downtown. You may own the company, but the company owns you, too.

Believe me, I know. I was in the same situation.

When I first started my business, I took on a ton of debt: ten times more risk than I ever imagined. Sure, I was proud of the leap I'd made, the vote of confidence in my capabilities. But, as my company grew, I was working more and more hours. I had employees, but they needed me to stand over their shoulder. My clients needed me, too. My company was completely dependent upon my time. And, thus, so was my income. I bought into a lie.

The Cashflow Quadrant is a useful model that helped me frame what it means to be a business owner. But what Kiyosaki failed to cover is a practical way to transition yourself from Self-Employed to Business Owner. He offers advice like 'hire smart people' and 'lead people'. That's great, but it's hard to think about doing any of that when you're already working 14-hour days.

I don't profess to have all the answers, but I've found a method that has worked for me and my clients. It begins by reframing what it means to be an entrepreneur. It's a foundational principle that I call 'Making Yourself Redundant'. You want to make yourself redundant from the daily operations of your business, so it's not dependent on you. And knowing your numbers helps a lot.

Your Business is Not Your Baby

I've heard an analogy that growing a business is akin to raising a child. We conceive it by registering a company. It starts to crawl, in some fashion, as we sign our first customer. It learns to walk as we employ staff.

We love it, nurture it, and devote our every waking hour to helping it mature.

But, often, the process itself is not pretty. Beneath the veil of a flashy website, the systems and people are hacked together. Loose ends and scrappy code can be cleaned up another day. We know it's not perfect, but it works—and it's ours. No matter how ugly and needy the baby might be, we give it a mother's unconditional love.

As time passes, we become more experienced as a parent and entrepreneur and, like a child, the business begins to sustain itself. Every parent knows that children don't stay small forever, and eventually your business should outgrow you as well.

I hear so many CEOs romanticize business as being like family. They try to instill a culture of unity and closeness, building a bubble of safety and nurturing. They treat their business like an extension of their real family. They think of it as their baby.

But it's not. Besides being emotionally misleading, the analogy is just plain wrong. Your business is not your baby.

Your real walking, talking child is your baby. You should direct your love and attachment to them. As for the family analogy... Well, if your family is anything like mine, they are dysfunctional.

It's easy to liken our business to family. I get it. The company you created is, literally, a manifestation of yourself—your way of seeing the world, your contribution to make it better.

But I prefer to frame business as something less emotive and, frankly, less complicated.

To me, business is more like a machine.

How to Design Your Machine

Ray Dalio, chairman and founder of the investment management firm Bridgewater Associates, is one of the world's most successful investors and entrepreneurs. Referred to as the 'Steve Jobs' of investing, Dalio is best known for his collective set of life and business principles which he recently collected into a book titled, simply enough, *Principles*.

One of Dalio's key messages is that effective entrepreneurs think about their businesses, not as children, but as machines.

He writes that "the most successful entrepreneurs are the ones that have 'higher thinking' and can take a step back and design a machine consisting of the right people doing the right things."

The Man Machine

Entrepreneurs that excel at higher thinking are able to objectively assess and improve their machine. You want to constantly compare the outcomes you're getting to the goals that you've set.

Take a look at the Machine Man sketch on the next page. Let's break it a down a bit.

The Machine can be visually represented as a feedback loop. The Goals are the driver to the machine, and the machine will produce the Outcomes. As the outcomes are achieved, new goals will be established. As those new outcomes are achieved, new goals are established. And it becomes a perpetuating cycle.

The Design includes your people, the culture you build, and the systems you rely upon. This unique combination is the engine of your machine, and can vary over time depending upon your goals. For example, if your goal is to build a new software product, you will need a setup that includes product design lead, an army of developers, and a product manager.

Simply put, as your objectives change, you must 'modify' your machine so that it is optimized for the right goal.

As an entrepreneur, you are the smiley guy at the top. Your goal as the visionary—the designer behind it all—is to build principles and systems that successfully produce the objectives of the business without it being dependent on you.

You have the controls to this machine and you must act accordingly. Your time and energy should not be spent spinning the cogs. Rather, your most valuable contribution is as the operator: constantly engineering, tinkering, and optimizing the machine to produce the outcomes you want.

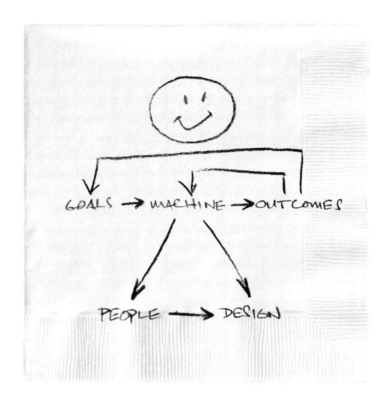

The Practicalities of Higher Thinking

Framing your business as a machine serves two purposes. Firstly, it will help to dismiss the deep heart-felt emotions that should be reserved for family and loved ones. It removes our attachment to our business and equips us to adopt a posture of 'higher thinking'. We remove our mind from the daily battles, so we can step back and view things from a mountain top—objectively crafting and strategizing our next move. Simply put, it's a mental model that provides us with perspective.

This framing serves to balance long-term thinking with present day happiness. In the startup phase, your machine inevitably begins as just one lonely cog. As you grow and add more parts to your machine, it's natural to be caught in a cycle of continually looking up—planning the number of parts you need to add to succeed. This can be intimidating and mentally exhausting.

Higher thinking allows us to reflect for a moment and take satisfaction in the machine we've built. Like a builder handcrafting her first home, you're able to picture the different parts that form your business. This visualization can offer a sense of satisfaction and gratitude, a mental model we can lean upon in times of overwhelm and anxiety.

You Build a Machine (But Don't Become It)

Michael Gerber, author of *The E-Myth*, says that all entrepreneurs are business owners, but not all business owners are entrepreneurs. Allow me to explain this statement, because it's important that we distinguish the two concepts.

An entrepreneur is a machine builder. She creates a vision, validates a product or service, employs people to fulfill that service, and expands it. The primary goal of the entrepreneur is to scale herself from the business, so it is not dependent on her time—to create a machine that grows and sustains itself.

The majority of independent business owners are not machine builders; they are the machine! They are the sole cog relentlessly spinning, trying to do paid work. If they do not do the work, they do not get paid. Yes, they may operate out of a company structure, have a logo, and employ some staff—but, fundamentally, they are still the machine.

Consider Brendan, the founder of the high-touch business, Voltage Media. Brendan does great work. He has great clients, and a team of 15 employees. Moreover, the firm is profitable.

But, after two long years of spinning cogs, Brendan is burning out. He needs his weekends back to spend time with the family. He needs a vacation to recharge. But Brendan can't afford to do any of those things, because as soon as he stops spinning cogs his income stops, too.

All of Voltage Media's clients are dependent on Brendan to be there cranking the gears, and he's dependent on them. Brendan has built himself a good job, not a great business.

Entrepreneurs, on the other hand, construct an entity far bigger than themselves. They design the machine so it's not dependent on their time. Instead of working in the business, they work on it. They make money while they sleep. They build a business they hope one day they'll be able to sell.

Henry Ford didn't make cars. He built a machine that, to this day, manufactures and sells cars. Jeff Bezos does not sell books, he's built an empire that sells everything. These are examples of entrepreneurs. They don't get stuck in sales, marketing, or product development—whatever part of the business they love. They build organizations that function without them. Your goal as an entrepreneur is to do the same.

Ask yourself what type of business owner you are. Are you an entrepreneur or a freelancer? If you're reading this book, chances are you're an entrepreneur—or want to be. But what if you're stuck just like Brendan? Relentlessly running on a hamster wheel, trying to keep it all from falling apart? That's okay, too. All entrepreneurs start there in one form or another. What matters is mindset.

Scaling Yourself From Your Machine

Escaping the treadmill, going from a self-employed cog spinner to an entrepreneurial machine builder, is a messy and difficult path. When you begin as the sole operator, you literally do everything— from the sales and marketing to managing employees and sweeping the floors. In this phase, it's hard to initially foresee yourself levelling up and adding more parts to your machine; you are the alpha and the omega.

The first step to building the machine is employing others to take over functions of the business. You may already be doing this. Is it working as smoothly and quickly as you hoped?

Whenever I seemed to get a leg up—taking three steps forward —there were inevitably two steps back. Take my staff, for instance. No, really—take them. Sometimes, I swear, I didn't know what they were doing. I expected a few headaches managing people, but honestly there were plenty of times that it seemed faster and easier to just do a task myself (rather than explain it again and again).

I'm sure you know that frustration, too. It's part of the business building process. Shake it off. And get in there and try a new angle.

In this stage of development, you need to focus on building repeatable systems—literally step-by-step breakdowns—so that new employees can seamlessly integrate into your expanding machine. The objective is to continually add parts and level yourself up, so that you are able to focus your time on higher leverage activities.

"If your business depends on you, you don't own a business, you have a job. And it's the worst job in the world because you're working for a lunatic."

Michael Gerber

THE 6 STAGES OF OWNERSHIP

Jason, the Technician

I was an employee for the majority of my career as an accountant. Despite various side hustles, I always relied on a steady paycheck from my employers. When I leaped into my business, I thought everything would change for the better. That was a false notion.

Instead of a nice swanky riverside office, I had a kitchen table. Instead of a team of people to rely on, it was just me and my business partner. I quickly realized that I was an S in the Cashflow Quadrant, not a B. I didn't own a business. I owned a job.

The first two years were the hardest. I did everything: sales, client management, hiring, marketing, building systems, and the actual work! In fact, looking back I'm not sure how on earth I was able to manage it all.

Oh, now I remember. Poorly. I managed it all poorly.

Trained as a technical accountant and advisor my entire career, my focus was on perfectionism. Clients paid us upwards of $1,000 an hour for our advice and work. If they picked up any error, no matter how small, it was a big deal. Reputation was everything, so I had to keep that perfectionist mentality for the technical work. The quality of the underlying product or service could not be sacrificed.

The problem was that I was holding onto that perfectionism mentality in other areas of the business.

People Don't Scale, But Systems Do

The thing I had to accept was letting go. Delegate and spend my time building systems and principles, so I could scale our growth and reduce my daily footprint in the company. I began to focus on making myself redundant.

Moving from technician to business owner was a big change in mindset. After completing some key hires to be in charge of the operations side of the business, my to-do list started to transform. Actually, it disappeared. My calendar was suddenly free, too.

I felt lost, like I had lost my identity. For my entire professional career I had always been focused on the technical work, now that I was no longer doing that, how was I supposed to spend my time?

A Quick Lesson on Higher Leverage Activities

In 1995 Andy Grove, the former CEO of Intel, wrote a book called *High Output Management*. It's regarded as the 'management bible' in Silicon Valley.

One of Grove's key themes is that for organizations to produce a productive and high-performing team, leaders and managers must focus their time on high-leverage activities.

So what activities are high leverage? Basically anything that sets up a team, or individual, for success over the long term. Grove says that high-leverage activities can be achieved in three ways:

- When many people are affected by one manager.

- When a person's activity over a long period of time is affected by a managers' brief, well-focused set of words or actions.

- When the work of a large group is affected by an individual supplying a unique, key piece of knowledge or information.

In short, you need to focus your time on gathering information, coaching, and leading people. If you're stuck in your business, it's hard to do any of that. You need to scale yourself from the grinding daily tasks as quickly as possible.

Spend your time designing and building systems so you can manage them, not be them.

Focusing on Higher Level Activities

I went back to the Andy Grove model of High Leverage Activities and challenged myself to track the activities I did on a day-to-day basis in order to use more of my time creating leverage.

So, for me, the first instance where I wanted more influence was marketing. Spreading the vision of our business to the market so that potential customers and staff were familiar with whom we were. From an internal perspective, my role transformed from a manager to coach—helping my staff become the best version of themselves. Now, three years after establishing my company, that's where I spend 95% of my time. Working *on* my business, not *in* it.

I find it ironic that, before I started my own business, I spent so much time in the boardrooms of large companies (and the kitchens of startups) advising them on financial strategy. The reality is that, as an employee, I lacked the empathy to understand the challenges that founders and entrepreneurs faced. A lot of the 'advice' I gave was fluff—over-engineered jargon to justify my old firm's big fees.

It was only after I began to practice what I preached that I realized what actually works.

The tactics I share in this Principle have helped me immensely.

The Business Owner Pyramid

In every business, there are six stages that every owner and founder moves through as she builds her machine. The stages are presented in the Business Owner Pyramid on the next page.

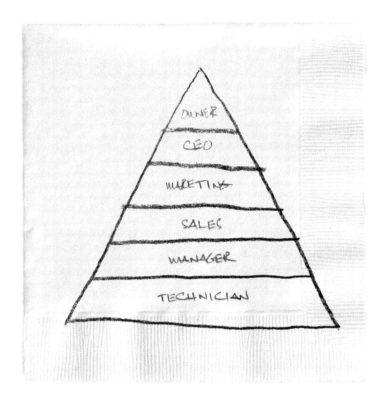

I'm going to assume you already play the role of the CEO, but you share one (or all) of these jobs within the Business Owner Pyramid. While it's likely you wear multiple hats every day, the point here is knowing where you should spend the majority of your time—leveraging your impact across the entire organization.

Let's start from the bottom.

STAGE 1 – THE TECHNICIAN

The Technician does the work being sold to customers. These are the folks who make the product, fulfill the service, and support your customers. They are responsible for delivering whatever it is people buy from you.

In the early days of Apple Computer, Steve Wozniak was the technician. The lawyer in her upstart law firm is a technician; so is the solopreneur graphic designer. In fact, the vast majority of independent business owners are technicians.

If the work stops, the money stops.

STAGE 2 – THE MANAGER

The Manager is responsible for supervising the technicians. She is in charge of ensuring the work gets done on spec and on budget. Managers spend the majority of their time on operations, quality assurance, coaching, and leading a team of technicians.

STAGE 3 – THE SALESPERSON

While the previous two roles are focused inwardly on the company, the Salesperson is outward-facing—connecting with the world at large. This person identifies business opportunities, generates leads, develops relationships, and closes deals.

STAGE 4 – THE MARKETER

The Marketer is responsible for spreading the vision of the organization. They tell the story of the business to the right people in the right way.

STAGE 5 – THE CEO

The CEO is responsible for everything in the company. Whether you're a one-person business or have a hundred employees, this is you. You're in charge.

But if you're still stuck spending too much time (really, any time at all) in the prior four roles, you haven't graduated completely to the C-suite.

A full-time CEO makes the day-to-day decisions that impact the entire company—implementing both short-term and long-term goals. The CEO is the conduit between the owners of the company and the management team.

STAGE 6 – THE OWNER

The peak of the pyramid is nirvana for every person who starts a business. The Owner is the investor. She receives financial returns from the performance of the business without direct involvement in the day-to-day management and running of the business.

The CEO will report to the owner on the overall performance of the business. As an owner, real wealth is generated via payments of profits and value creation of the company.

Your Place in the Pyramid

Which of these roles you inhabit is largely dependent upon your business objectives, and your initial cash position.

For example, if you've raised money from investors, you'll have the funds to hire Technicians and play the role of the Manager or Marketer right away. This is where Sarah, the founder of our low-touch business model Moo Formula, is placed. She has a team and a system to produce and sell her product. Her role is to manage and improve it.

If you're self-funded (or 'bootstrapped' in startup jargon), you may need to start as Technician and graduate yourself upward—just like Brendan did.

In order to scale yourself up the business—to spend your time solely as CEO and owner—you need an intimate understanding of your business model and its financial drivers. The numbers leave clues on how best to spend your limited resources in order to efficiently grow your machine.

However, as you scale yourself up the company, you may lose visibility over what's actually happening. The quantification of key performance indicators can provide you with an objective tool to measure the effectiveness of the systems you develop. This ensures that the people replacing your roles in the lower stages are not only doing their job well, but are doing it *better* than you ever could.

We will uncover these numbers in latter parts of this book—answering common questions like how to know when you should employ your next staff member, and what indicators you should measure to manage a new hire's effectiveness.

But, before we talk about paying other people, I want to cover a crucial topic: paying yourself something first.

The Two Financial Hats

Let's look deeper at what it means to be the owner and the CEO. Simply put, one owns the machine and the other operates it.

As the owner, you wear an investor hat. The investor considers the startup capital injected just like the shares bought on the stock market or real-estate investments. You want to ensure the capital and time invested in your wealth-creating machine will provide you with a financial return in the future.

As the CEO, you wear an employee hat. Your role is to operate the business and ensure it's well managed financially.

These two roles will conflict.

As the owner, your motivation is to maximize the financial return from your business. To generate a return on the investment of capital and time you have contributed while building it.

The dilemma you will face is the trade-off between taking income now as a CEO versus long-term wealth creation for your role as an investor. You earn present income from the salary you make as an employee, as well as dividends the business may pay yourself as an investor.

Yet, the more present income you draw from the business now, the less capital there is to invest in the business to create long-term value. On the other hand, drawing the minimal amount of present income leaves more capital to create higher long-term value (if re-invested wisely), but at the cost to your current standard of living outside of the business.

And, quite often, you're not making this decision in a vacuum. You might have a life partner and even a family to consider, as well.

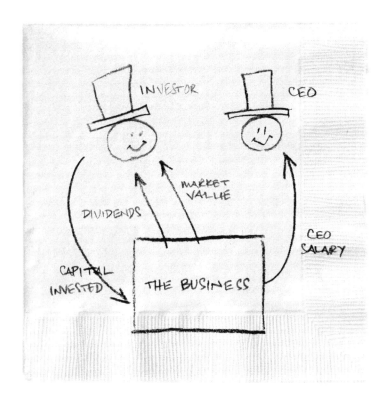

Now, I am not suggesting that you have to be a sadist or masochist to be an entrepreneur (although it's likely that many are). My point is there are trade-offs that you, as both an owner and CEO, need to make. This applies to your lifestyle, too.

Paying Yourself First

Nike, now the titan of the sporting apparel world, was spawned from an idea not dissimilar to yours or mine—dissatisfaction with the status quo. Founded by track athlete Phil Knight, he turned his frustration with running shoes availability in the early 1970s into the billion dollar empire it is today. Like all great successes, it didn't happen overnight.

In his memoir *Shoe Dog*, Knight shares his business struggles in its startup years. "The business simply couldn't support me," he writes. "Though the company was on track to double sales for a fifth straight year, it still couldn't justify a salary for its cofounder."

Despite running a multi-million dollar company, with team members spread across the country, Knight still held a full-time job as a CPA accountant to pay the bills in his personal life. How's that for a serving of humble pie?

Now consider Brendan, our founder of the high-touch business Voltage Media. He's working 90 hours a week to get his company off the ground. Despite the huge time commitment, he's not paying himself anything close to what he was earning at his previous job. And his personal financial situation is suffering as a result of it.

Brendan is in a quandary.

Should he invest more money into the business by hiring more staff, with the aim of scaling himself out of the technician work? Surely, having more staff will free up his personal time for a better quality of life.

Or, should he save the money and pay himself a higher salary now instead?

The former means he may work less hours, allowing him to build systems and financial value in the business. But, the trade-off is a below average, short-term personal financial situation.

The other option is to pay himself more now—which means higher personal income, but will certainly result in working longer hours, and a higher chance that his disgruntled wife will divorce him. It's quite a pickle.

What we know for certain is that Brendan won't be able to draw a 'market value' salary during his startup phase. You can't have your cake and eat it, too.

Remember, your objective is to scale yourself from the business. It's unlikely you'll have the resources to support an industry comparable income while investing cash flow into what the business needs to be self-sustaining. If getting paid top dollar right out of the gate is your priority, then perhaps you're better suited to freelancing or contracting or, dare I say it, employment.

The art is finding a balance that gives you enough present income to support the lifestyle you need, while still providing the business with the funds it needs to fuel healthy growth.

So, what's a realistic, happy middle ground for your salary? Here's a methodology to try: it's called Minimum Viable Lifestyle.

"One can furnish a room very luxuriously by taking out furniture rather than putting it in."

Francis Jourdian

MINIMUM VIABLE LIFESTYLE

What's an MVL?

You may be familiar with the Silicon Valley term Minimal Viable Product (MVP). This phrase was popularized by startup guru Eric Ries in his legendary book *The Lean Startup*. The MVP thesis is designed around building the cheapest and smallest product possible, with just enough features to satisfy your early customers. The idea is to work within a cost constraint that achieves the most viable outcome.

The MVP principle can be adapted to disciplines outside of the software and product development world. As an accountant, I like to apply this perspective to my personal finances. Let's call this exercise the Minimum Viable Lifestyle (MVL).

The idea behind the MVL is to design your lifestyle so that you are living on the lowest viable cost, which still yields the highest impact to your satisfaction. The core principle is that you only spend money on things which have a high personal utility.

The process involves an audit of your personal monthly lifestyle expenses, and eliminating the unnecessary or impulse purchases. The aim is to understand the minimum salary you can live off of and still enjoy a satisfactory life.

From a business accounting perspective, figuring out your MVL provides a guide of what monthly salary you should draw before investing any surplus profit back into the business. Remember, we want to make sure that you pay yourself first, so your personal finances don't suffer.

Now before I scare the crap out of you, I want to emphasize that the key word here is 'satisfactory'. An MVL does not mean poverty. It simply means making small sacrifices that still provide you a comfortable quality of life. You want to be disciplined about leaving enough cash flow in your business so that it can thrive, too.

Here's how to do it.

Calculating Your MVL

First, put everything on the table. The more expenses and receipts you consider, the better you'll understand your own number.

STEP 1 – REVIEW YOUR SPENDING

Take a look at your personal bank and credit card statements for the last month and tally your spending into four categories: 1) food and entertainment, 2) housing, 3) transportation, and 4) well, that's everything else.

Setup a spreadsheet and enter them into columns. To help you categorize these items, here's a list of the most common expenses and where they should be allocated in your lifestyle expenses.

FOOD AND ENTERTAINMENT
- Groceries
- Netflix/Spotify subscriptions
- Restaurants
- Gifts

HOUSING
- Mortgage repayments
- Rent
- Utilities

TRANSPORTATION
- Car repayments
- Car insurance and registration
- Fuel
- Public transport
- Taxis and ride-sharing

EVERYTHING ELSE
- Health insurance
- Childcare expenses
- Tuition
- Self education expenses
- Medical expenses

There may be expenses that don't directly fit into these buckets. To make this easy, just put them into an 'other' category. The objective here is not extreme detail in the categories; it's simply to get a base understanding of your current lifestyle costs.

STEP 2 – CONDUCT A LIFESTYLE REVIEW

Now that you've got a summary of your current living expenses, work with your 'significant other' (partner, husband, wife, etc.) and review the cost buckets. Ask yourself, which are really necessary? If we go without them, how would that impact our happiness?

I'm not suggesting you be a scrooge here. Your MVL should be the bare minimum of costs to live a comfortable life. Be realistic.

Usually, the biggest gains can be found in the food and entertainment bucket. Think about how small changes can impact your costs. It could be as simple as moving 'date night' out to once a month, instead of once a week. Remember, the less you can live on, the more you can invest back into your business.

Once you've identified the 'unnecessary' expenses, remove them from the total and re-calculate your monthly lifestyle expenses. This is your new MVL budget.

STEP 3 – ADD A BUFFER

After totalling your revised lifestyle expenses, add a 30% margin to factor personal taxes and a savings safety net. This is your fund for 'rainy days'. This final number is your monthly MVL.

MVL Expenses

Housing	$2,000
Food and Entertainment	$1,500
Transport	$1,500
Health, Childcare, and Education	$2,000
Sub Total	$7,000
TOTAL (with 30% buffer)	$9,100

Your MVL value forms the monthly salary you should be drawing from your business in the startup phase. If you're drawing over and above this monthly salary and your business can support it, then it's okay to leave it. As long as your current salary is not constraining the potential for the business to grow.

If your current salary is below this MVL, maybe you can use this calculation as a justification to give yourself a bit of a raise.

When You Should Reinvest into Your Business

Before reinvesting every dollar of profit back into your business, it's important to ensure that first you're paying your MVL to live a comfortable personal life. The challenge is knowing what business revenue you need to reach in order to generate this extra profit.

We can better understand this number by calculating your MVL break-even point.

Your Business Break-Even Point

You may be familiar with business term 'break-even point' which calculates the number of sales to be made (in dollars or units), before all the business expenses are covered and profit begins.

You can calculate this by dividing your fixed overhead expenses by your contribution margin.

BREAK-EVEN = FIXED EXPENSES / CONTRIBUTION MARGIN

We'll dive deeper into these terms in Principle 2. But, for now, let's use Brendan's agency as an example.

Voltage Media has $155,000 of monthly fixed expenses, which includes Brendan's founder salary of $5,000 per month. The firm makes a 90% contribution margin on every sale.

The business break-even point is calculated as:

Break-even = $155,000 / (90%)
Break-even sales per month = $172,222

This means that Brendan needs to generate $172,222 per month in sales in order to reach break-even on his costs. Note this figure includes the $5K per month salary that he pays himself.

Knowing your break-even point is vital, and serves its purpose from an accounting perspective. It helps you understand the sales your company must generate to start (or keep) making a profit.

But, for the purposes of understanding the balancing act between personal and business cash flow, it is flawed. Why? Well, firstly, the salary you are drawing from the business is probably really low (way below market value), which skews the business break-even point calculation. Secondly, it doesn't factor in your personal expenses outside of the business.

To quantify the sales needed to pay yourself enough to fund a satisfactory lifestyle, we need a break-even calculation which considers both your business and personal lifestyle expenses.

This is where we incorporate your MVL salary into the break-even point equation. The MVL break-even point helps you understand the revenue your company must generate in order to cover your business expenses and MVL salary.

It serves as a benchmark revenue number for a bootstrapped founder to understand at what point their startup will generate enough revenue to pay for a satisfactory salary—before reinvesting everything back into growth.

How to Calculate Your MVL Break-Even Point

Let's get a bit more into the weeds here.

To calculate a break-even point for your MVL, we'll first deduct your current salary from the overhead costs of your business. Then, we'll add the lifestyle expenses (you already calculated) to your overhead expenses and use this to calculate your final break-even.

STEP 1 – CALCULATE YOUR TOTAL MONTHLY EXPENSES

This means everything to support your lifestyle. And, just to be on the safe side, I suggest that you include a 30% margin:

MVL Expenses

Housing	$2,000
Food and Entertainment	$1,500
Transport	$1,500
Health, Childcare, and Education	$2,000
Sub Total	$7,000
TOTAL (with 30% buffer)	**$9,100**

STEP 2 – DEDUCT YOUR SALARY FROM FIXED EXPENSES

Start with your total business fixed costs (again on a monthly basis), then subtract your current monthly salary:

Business fixed costs:	$155,000 per month
Less founder salary:	($5,000) per month
Adjusted business fixed costs:	$150,000 per month

STEP 3 – ADD YOUR LIFESTYLE EXPENSES TO FIXED EXPENSES

Now we're going to add the lifestyle expenses you calculated to your adjusted fixed costs. We'll use this value to calculate your lifestyle break-even.

Adjusted business fixed costs:	$150,000 per month
Add lifestyle expenses:	$9,100 per month
Total business and lifestyle expenses:	$159,100 per month

The recalculated business break-even point is calculated as:

Break-even = $159,100 / (90%)
Break-even sales per month = $176,778

This means that Brendan needs to generate at least $176,778 of sales per month to break-even on his business expenses, and cover his MVL at the same time.

Having a lifestyle break-even point provides a guide of the minimum sales required to cover your MVL. It represents a target of how much in sales dollars you should generate before reinvesting the surplus profit back into the business for growth and hiring—while ensuring a satisfactory lifestyle outside of the business.

One last important thing to note: this lifestyle break-even calculation assumes just one founder. If there are more than one of you in the business, you will need to cater for them as well.

Revising and Reviewing Your MVL

Of course, your personal circumstances will continually change and evolve. Set time to review your MVL on an annual basis to ensure your salary is keeping up with the expenses in your personal life.

Similarly, the MVL is a calculation used for startups and high-growth businesses where every spare dollar is invested into the business for growth and expansion. At some point, your business will hit a maturity level, where sales and profit margins will (hopefully) remain strong and constant.

In this phase, you can look at revising your MVL upwards to give yourself a higher standard of living. To help you calculate it, you can simply add a new cost category to your MVL called 'bonus lifestyle expenses'.

Discipline With the Two Financial Hats

As the owner of your business machine, you will be tempted to pinch money from your company bank account. It's common to see business owners finance their personal mortgages, cars, and even family holidays via their company bank account.

You're probably thinking what's so wrong with that? After all, you're the CEO and owner. It's your money, right?

This is a common misinterpretation. We need to keep in mind that business and personal expenses are separate. The added benefit of calculating your MVL salary is that it mentally draws a line in the sand. Rather than taking money from the business as you need it, it helps you to stick to a fixed monthly salary. Surplus profit in the company should be paid as a dividend, not for you to pinch when you feel fit.

In short, the only cash you should take from your company is via your salary. Anything above that number should be paid via a distribution of profit.

You Have the Controls to Your Machine

In summary, you, the entrepreneur wear two hats: an investor hat and a CEO hat. In the decision-making process, it's important to respect that these roles will be in conflict. There are trade-offs we all make, and—while sometimes it may not feel as such—you do have the controls to make change happen.

"Infinitely more important than sharing one's material wealth is sharing the wealth of ourselves—our time and energy, our passion and commitment, and, above all, our love."

William E. Simon

YOUR BUSINESS IS YOUR OTHER SPOUSE

Entrepreneurs are from All Walks of Life

Stories of entrepreneurship are akin to the hero's journey you read about in fairy tales. The protagonist embarks on a bold quest to slay some sort of dragon; he goes through a series of trials and tribulations; then there's a happy ending.

In entrepreneur land, the popular mythology goes a little something like my sketch on the next page.

We start with a couple of college kids in their dorm room (or maybe it's their first apartment after graduation). The brilliant young founders stumble across a 'disruptive' idea for an app. One guy can code the backend; the other guy can design the frontend. They build a quick prototype and push it out to a small group of friends for beta testing.

Now, armed with a group of 'dedicated' users, they pitch said idea to investors. Every slide in their deck is a masterful work of art; the art of persuasion, that is.

They raise a bucket load of money, go through a series of trials and tribulations, blah blah blah. Then, within two years, they make bank in a huge exit/acquisition. In the end, with neither one barely 25-years-old, they 'retire' to become venture capitalists.

The Myth of the Garage (or Apartment) Startup

Let's take the story of AirBnB as an example.

Once upon a time, two 27-year-old college friends struggled to pay rent in their apartment in downtown San Francisco. There was a design conference coming to town and all the city hotels were booked out. Jumping on this opportunity to earn a few extra dollars to make rent, they hacked together a website and turned their apartment into a bed and breakfast. They spent their waking hours building out the website and platform of Airbnb for several years. After a series of setbacks and wins, they got traction and are now the billion-dollar unicorn we see today.

Consider Elon Musk and his brother Kimbal building their first startup, Zip2, in the mid-90's. Surviving off a loan provided by their uncle, the Musk brothers lived and slept in their office—surviving on takeaway for the first two years. After a series of struggles, they got funding. Years later it sold to Compaq Computers for $307M.

Tales of entrepreneurship are often about the 'struggle' of two single white guys in Silicon Valley, building a business out of their apartment or garage. They come up with an idea and work their asses off for 15 hours a day—living off ramen noodles—in the hope that they'll 'get funding'.

The problem I have is that these stories are outliers. According to Forbes, 80% of businesses fail. We don't often hear stories of that 80%. Out of sight, out of mind?

Indeed, we can aspire to be like our heroes. We rely on these stories to give us the irrational optimism to believe that we can be just like Jobs and Wozniak, or the Musk brothers. But reality is that the odds are against us. And if we're not grounded in facts, we can be caught in a fairy tale—where success is fiction.

The truth is that most entrepreneurs don't start businesses from their dorm room. They are professionals who have left employment to control their own destiny. They are ordinary people, like you and me. We don't fit one type of mold. We are all different, in different stages of life. We may have partners, children, mortgages, or elderly parents. Simply put, we have varying degrees of priorities outside of business.

These have a direct impact to our quality of life inside and outside of our company. When it comes to creating a successful life for ourselves, we need to consider the whole package.

Your Business is Your Other Partner

Starting a business is a selfish pursuit. You devote every waking hour into growing it. It's your life's work, literally. It can be easy for it to swallow you whole.

Entrepreneurs start companies to do their own thing. Marriage, on the other hand, is about doing things together. The truth is that these two loves of your life will forever be in conflict.

There is limited data on divorce statistics for entrepreneurs, but I'd wager that they are higher than the average. I'm grateful not to be in that bucket. Indeed the demands of my business occasionally has created periods of distance and pressure between my partner and I. It's a balance of give and take. At times, there is tension as we work within that constraint of time and attention.

And, of course, there's financial pressure. According to research by the University of Denver, financial problems are one of the leading causes of divorce.

Being a business owner requires a tolerance for financial risk that few can stomach. In a marriage or long-term relationship with shared finances, it's likely you'll need to tap into that joint bank account. The new car you promised will likely be deferred. The annual holiday, too. The sacrifices are not just yours. You, your partner, and your entire family are all in it together.

This raises some awkward, yet practical questions to consider between you and your spouse, including:

- How will I pay my fair share of the living expenses?
- If I can't, how will you pay for it?
- How are we going to save for the future?
- How long will I be able to give this thing a go?
- What's the backup plan?

Relationship breakdowns are a serious (yet seldom talked about) issue from the lens of entrepreneurship. I've seen marriages and homes destroyed because of business. Look at the personal lives of Musk or Jobs. They're not the ones I wish to emulate.

Equally, I've witnessed businesses destroyed by divorce. Divorce creates a great deal of psychological pressure on founders. I've seen founders forced to liquidate their business to pay their share. Want a sure way to lose 50% of your wealth overnight? Get a divorce.

With financial pressures as a leading cause of relationship breakdowns for founders, I'd like to offer a financial framework to help you engage in a purposeful discussion.

Before we start, let me be clear. I am not a therapist or marriage counsellor. But from my own experience, dealing with the financial elephant in the room is generally the hardest and most important conversation for early-stage business owners.

Here's how to approach it.

STEP 1 – CALCULATE YOUR MUTUAL MVL

Sit down with your significant other and calculate your mutual MVL. When I say mutual, I mean the total lifestyle and living expenses for your whole family. You can go back and follow the steps detailed in the previous chapter, Minimum Viable Lifestyle.

STEP 2 – DISCUSS YOUR 'FAIR SHARE'

If your household is like mine, we split our living costs 50/50. We have a joint bank account for the mortgage, utilities, car, (and such), and top-up this account every month to cover our 'fair share'.

The challenge you may face in your early-stage company is that your contribution will no longer be 'fair'. It's likely you will have to lean on your partner, financially (and emotionally) to foot the bill to maintain your lifestyle. This raises an important question: How much *can* you lean on them?

There is no right or wrong answer. But it does need a real, honest discussion about how much each of you can contribute.

After calculating your MVL, sit down and calculate what each of you can afford to contribute to the household.

Using Brendan's example, his family's mutual MVL is $9,100 per month.

MVL Expenses

Housing	$2,000
Food and Entertainment	$1,500
Transport	$1,500
Health, Childcare, and Education	$2,000
Sub Total	$7,000
TOTAL (with 30% buffer)	$9,100

The discussion Brendan needs to have with his wife is: How do we fund that?

In this situation, Brendan is able to draw $5,000 per month as a salary from Voltage Media, so he's able to cover 55% of this share to the household. This leaves his wife $4,100 to contribute.

Fair Share Contribution

Brendan	$5,000	55 %
Brendan's Wife	$4,100	45 %
TOTAL	$9,100	

STEP 3 – CALCULATE YOUR PERSONAL RUNWAY

In Brendan's example, we saw that both Brendan and his wife could cover their MVL. But what if Brendan's wife wasn't working, and instead took care of the children full-time?

Fair Share Contribution

Brendan	$5,000	55 %
Brendan's Wife	$0	0 %
TOTAL	$5,000	
MVL Shortfall	($4,100)	

Herein lies the predicament: there's a shortfall. Brendan and his wife must dip into their personal savings to fund their lifestyle.

Your 'personal runway' is the amount of time (in months) you have to fund your MVL with the savings you've accumulated in your personal life.

This is a different concept from the runway in your business (we'll explore that further in Principle 3). Remember, the business bank account is separate from your personal bank account.

Calculating Your Personal Runway

You can calculate your personal runway by getting the shortfall to the monthly MVL and dividing it by the current savings you have.

Let's say that, at this point, Brendan and his wife have $23,000 of savings. Brendan accessed some home equity to fund the startup of Voltage Media, and had some money set aside for 'rainy days'.

Under these circumstances, Brendan and his wife have about six months until they deplete their savings.

Personal Runway Calculation

Current Savings	$23,000
MVL Shortfall	($4,100)
Personal Runway	6 Months

Should Brendan and his wife be concerned? I recommend that every household have at least six months of personal runway in the bank. They should take this half-year window into consideration.

Brendan's scenario opens a basket of questions, including:

- Can Brendan and his wife cut their living expenses more?
- Should Brendan's wife go back to employment?
- When should Brendan just quit the business and get a job?

How Long Do We Keep this Thing Going?

The ultimate question for Brendan to consider is how long is he willing keep working at Voltage Media. How long should he pursue the dream and grow the company's revenues? Does he have enough time to increase Voltage's cash flow and pay himself a higher salary?

Again, there is no easy answer. It requires an open conversation with his wife about how long they continue along this path.

Couples fight about money all the time, and with added stresses of business, there will always be conflicting priorities. I've seen stories (too many times) of founders falling in love with their business to the extent that it damages their personal relationships. Just be open and realistic about the life you want to live.

Optimism Bias

When I started my business, I was confident I'd be able to replace my income within 18 months. Four years later, I'm still not there. Why? Because I'm reinvesting everything back in.

As entrepreneurs, we are naturally optimistic (remember the reality distortion field?). Don't let this bias consume your process around drawing a wage from your business. Be realistic and try to err on the conservative side. This exercise is about expectation management with your partner. It's not a sales pitch to investors.

Framing Your Fair Share

In stereotypical households, there is a breadwinner: the person that earns the higher salary and contributes the most to the household. If that breadwinner isn't bringing home the bacon because she's investing everything into her 'hungry' early-stage business, there's a psychological aspect to consider.

Knowing that you're not contributing enough to the household can hurt your self-esteem. Couple this with the ordinary stress of shepherding a new company, and it's a heavy emotional burden.

I've seen couples deal with this issue in novel ways by reframing the meaning of 'fair share'. One example is that the partner with steady employment can cover the day-to-day living costs, while the partner with the young business take care of the 'special treats', like vacations, holidays, and birthday presents. Defining your fair share will help you feel that you're still contributing to the household in a meaningful and impactful way.

Glass and Rubber Balls

To hammer home this important point, Bryan Dyson, the ex-CEO of Coca-Cola, discussed the difference between two types of balls:

> *"Imagine life as a game in which you are juggling some five balls in the air. You name them: work, family, health, friends, and spirit. And you're keeping all of these in the air. You will soon understand that work is a rubber ball. If you drop it, it will bounce back.*
>
> *But the other four balls—family, health, friends, and spirit—are made of glass. If you drop one of these, they will be irrevocably scuffed, marked, nicked, damaged, or even shattered. They will never be the same. You must understand that and strive for balance in your life."*

Life is about trade-offs. If you say 'yes' to work and business, what are you saying 'no' to?

Business can be an all-consuming pursuit and we need to devote our attention to it in order to be successful. But we also need to be careful not to let it swallow us whole. Remember your business is simply a vehicle, a machine. This machine is designed to produce the outcomes you want.

You are in control.

In our next Principle, we will explore the financial controls to your business. The financial levers you can pull and flex to architect the outcomes you desire.

Principle 1 Takeaways

- Your business is a machine—and you have the controls to it. Spend your time as the operator and continually engineer, tinker, and optimize it to produce the outcomes you want.

- As an entrepreneur, your objective is to scale yourself from your machine—having an intimate understanding of your business and financial drivers is critical to help you do this.

- As a leader and manager, focus spending your time on high leverage activities.

- You wear two financial hats: business owner and CEO.

- To work out how much to pay yourself as a startup, consider calculating your Minimum Viable Lifestyle (MVL). It'll help you set a benchmark of when you can afford to reinvest profit back into growing your machine.

- Knowing your break-even point can help you understand the sales required to cover your business expenses. Factoring in your MVL gives you a 'whole of life' perspective to understand the sales required to cover both business and lifestyle costs.

- As the owner and CEO of your machine, you will be tempted to pinch extra money from the company bank account. Don't let this habit build. Remain disciplined, and know that you can pay profits via a dividend instead.

- Your business is your other spouse—don't neglect your real one! Have a realistic conversation about the financial consequences of your business—using the MVL framework as guidance.

- If you are 'burning money' in your household, be sure to calculate your personal runway to get real on when you should consider how long to keep this thing going.

MAXIMIZE YOUR MARGINS

REVENUE IS OVERRATED

Margins are what really matters. Learn the key profit
metrics that every entrepreneur should be measuring
and the tactical approaches to improve them.

"Many a false step was made by standing still."

Tim Ferriss

THE 3 PROFIT LEVERS

Profit Isn't Sexy: Revenue Is

When people ask me about growing and scaling their company, I hear a lot about growing revenue. In fact, the conversation is almost always focused on revenue.

"How do I efficiently scale sales? What's my month-on-month revenue growth compared to benchmarks? What's my CAGR?"

This is understandable. The media lavishes praise on companies that boast quadrillion-digit revenue growth, particularly in the tech startup world. As business owners, it's easy to be sucked into a vortex—an insular attitude where nothing but revenue growth matters. It's often perceived as the sole metric of 'success.'

But whatever happened to the humble profit margin? You know that quiet guy? The most important (yet rarely mentioned) aspect of business sitting patiently in the shadows. Perhaps you haven't seen him in a while.

Seldom do you hear media reports about companies growing their profitability. After all, profit isn't sexy: revenue is. Don't get me wrong, revenue growth is important. But, over the long term, what's a company worth if it only has revenue and not profit? Indeed we can look to tech companies like Uber and Snapchat as examples of highly-valued companies that are still posting billions of dollars of losses. I'm curious to see their market cap a decade from now.

My point is, revenue is important. But it's only one part of the equation. I think we should be talking more about margins, and less about revenue.

I'm referring to your company's ability to generate profit.

In this chapter, I will explain the core principles of how you can hack your financials to improve the profitability of your business.

Demystifying Profit

In the jargon of accounting speak, 'profit' can refer to many things. You may have heard the following phrases thrown around by your CPA or even the talking heads on Bloomberg. For them, profit is defined interchangeably as:

- Earnings
- EBIT (Earnings Before Interest and Tax)
- EBITDA (Earnings Before Interest, Tax, Deprec. & Amort.)
- NPBT (Net Profit Before Tax)
- NPAT (Net Profit After Tax)
- Net Income
- Net Margin

Believe it or not, some of these terms actually mean the same thing. Others don't. It's a minefield when trying to understand your financial position. Using them interchangeably can be deadly.

Rather than bore you with all the confusing jargon, I want to cut right to the chase. Here are the three most important types of profit that you need to understand:

- Gross Profit
- Net Profit
- Operating Profit (EBIT)

Let's start from the top.

Are You Selling Your Products at the Right Profit?

Gross Profit is a crucial metric that every entrepreneur should be measuring in their business. The purpose of measuring your gross profit is to give you an understanding of the profit you make at the level of individual products. That is, when you make a sale, what's the profit after all the direct costs are deducted.

It's important to measure gross profit because you want to understand what profit margin you're making on your products and services. You want to ensure you have enough remaining profit to reinvest back in your business.

The margin of your Gross Profit is calculated as Sales less your Direct Costs. It's typically expressed as a percentage. The percentage is simply your gross profit dollars divided by the sales for the period you're looking at.

$$GROSS\ PROFIT\ =\ SALES\ -\ DIRECT\ COSTS$$

Breaking Down Direct Costs

Direct Costs—also referred to as Cost of Goods Sold or Cost of Sales—are all the expenses that are attributed to the production of your product and service. This includes the costs of the materials, direct labor costs, software hosting, and shipping.

Direct costs can be further split into Variable and Fixed Costs. Variable costs are all the expenses that increase in direct relation to your sales volume. Examples include the costs of your product and all the associated shipping and logistics expenses (assuming you're an inventory-based business).

Fixed costs, on the other hand are all the expenses that will stay the same, irrespective of your volume. Fixed costs include the direct labor costs (in a service-based business), software hosting (for a software business), and most other expenses. General operating expenses are also fixed costs.

It's important to identify your fixed and variable costs because it helps you accurately calculate your break-even point.

In Principle 1, for example, we helped Brendan calculate his MVL break-even point. The formula we used was:

BREAK-EVEN = FIXED EXPENSES / CONTRIBUTION MARGIN

The key here is knowing your company's contribution margin, which is calculated as your your sales less direct variable costs.

CONTRIBUTION MARGIN = SALES – DIRECT VARIABLE COSTS

Contribution margin is important because it represents the total 'contribution' of profit available to pay for the firm's fixed expenses.

Gross profit is different than contribution margin because it includes both variable and fixed direct costs.

Here's a summary of Moo Formula's Gross Profit breakdown for the year ended 31 December 2017 to illustrate my point:

Gross Profit
Moo Formula Inc.
For the year ended 31 December 2017

	31-Dec-2017
REVENUE	$4,374,631
DIRECT COSTS	
Variable Costs	
Opening Stock	$1,000,000
Purchases	$3,012,242
Closing Stock	($1,500,000)
	$2,512,242
Contribution Margin	**$1,862,389**
	43 %
Fixed Costs	
Wages - direct costs	$550,000
Total Direct Costs	$3,062,242
Gross Profit	**$1,312,389**
	30 %

In the diagram on the previous page, you can see that Moo Formula makes a contribution margin of $1.862M (or 43%) which relates to all the variable product expenses. As the business continues to sell more volume, we would expect these expenses to grow in the same proportion.

The direct wages expenses of $550K are fixed expenses, because wages expenses will not grow on a per unit basis of new sales made.

An analysis of your contribution margin not only helps you to understand your break-even, it can also assist in pricing decisions. We explore this in depth later in the chapter.

Screw Sales. You Want More Gross Profit

We've all heard the cliche 'sales fix everything'. Business idols like author and speaker Grant Cardone incessantly focus on improving the topline: revenue. Indeed, sales fix a lot of problems. As long as you have sales, you have cash flow to invest in your team, tech, and sales & marketing. But like every piece of advice from business gurus, take it with a grain of salt.

Sales don't fix everything: gross profit dollars do. Let me explain.

A dollar is a dollar, right? One dollar of sales is the same in comparison to another? Not quite. Not all revenue dollars are created equal, but all gross profit dollars are. Personally, I think measuring gross profit is more important than sales, because it shows the quality of your sales.

Let's take Sarah's Moo Formula startup as an example.

The financial statements show the comparative sales, direct costs and gross profit margin from the 2016 and 2017 financial year end.

Looking solely at revenue, you could say that Moo Formula had considerable growth in 2017 compared to the previous year—it did an extra $625K of sales. However, examine each year's gross profit. You'll find the company actually generated less money than 2016.

Why? Because Sarah and her team didn't produce and sell their products as efficiently as the previous financial year. Although sales grew, gross profit actually declined. All the hard work they did was eroded by inefficiencies.

Profit & Loss
Moo Formula Inc.
For the year ended 31 December 2017

	31-Dec-2017	31-Dec-2016
Revenue	$4,374,631	$3,750,000
Direct Costs	$3,062,242	$2,100,000
Gross Profit	$1,312,389	$1,650,000
Gross Profit Margin	30 %	44 %

Sales don't fix everything. Having a high gross profit margin can give your business a competitive advantage because better gross profit margins are an indicator of efficiency.

If your goal is to increase profit and you haven't figured out how to produce your product efficiently, simply adding more sales will not result in more profit. In fact, it can have a reverse effect and create a fat, profit-eating monster. Bigger is not always better.

What is a Good Gross Profit?

Gross profit is a slippery animal. A high gross profit allows for more earnings to be reinvested back into the growth of your business, increasing areas such as sales and marketing. Alternatively, it can be used to pay a return to shareholders (like you, presumably).

However, when gross profit margins are too big, competitors can often sniff it out. They may start to duplicate what you're doing —looking for new methods to be faster and cheaper.

Amazon is a prime example of this. The company intentionally prices their products to operate on rock-bottom margins. It's their long-term strategy to win more customers and take market share.

In the words of Jeff Bezos, "Your margin is my opportunity".

Gross profit margins will vary depending upon the industry and market size. Software companies, for example, have high gross profit margins (around 70%-80%) compared to wholesalers that have low margins (closer to 30%).

The table below summarizes average gross profit margins for a few industry types—divided by high-touch versus low-touch:

High-Touch	Target Gross Profit Margins
Professional Services	65 %
Trades	50 %
Wholesale	30 %
Hospitality	40 %
Low-Touch	
Ecommerce / Retail	50 %
Software	80 %
Marketplace / Agency	20 %

Use this table as a guide to comparable businesses in your industry. It's a relatively good benchmark, but don't get too caught up by trying to be like everyone else. They are, after all, your competition. You may find that your target is different.

There is one exception to this rule, however, a time when you must listen to your gross profit margins: when they're negative! It means you are losing money on every sale. This indicates your business model is broken and needs to be changed.

Net Profit versus Operating Profit

Net Profit is the type of profit I'm sure you are all very familiar with. It's calculated as revenue less your total expenses. It's generally expressed as a percentage—by taking your net profit and dividing it by revenue.

Interestingly enough, there is a variation of net profit that you should also be paying attention to. It's known as Operating Profit, or EBIT. EBIT stands for Earnings Before Interest and Tax.

EBIT is the same as net profit, except it doesn't include your interest or your income tax expenses.

Why should you care about this?

When you want to understand the underlying financial performance of a business, you want to look at the operating profit. That is, the performance of the operations of your business.

The problem with net profit is that it doesn't give you enough clarity as it's skewed by taxes and interest expenses.

Let's compare two generic companies as an example:

Profit & Loss
For the year ended 31 December 2017

	Company A	Company B
Revenue	$5,000,000	$5,000,000
Direct Costs	$3,000,000	$3,000,000
Gross Profit	$2,000,000	$2,000,000
Operating Expenses	$1,500,000	$1,500,000
Operating Profit (EBIT)	$500,000	$500,000
Interest	$120,000	–
Income Tax	$150,000	$150,000
Net Profit	$230,000	$350,000

BANK FINANCING

NO INTEREST = FUNDED BY VC

While the companies have exactly the same operating profit, their net profit is different. Why? Because Company A has interest expenses since it's taken on debt from a bank. Company B, on the other hand, has received funding from a VC (at no interest).

If you looked solely at net profit, you would say that Company B is a better performing company than Company A. That's wrong. Fundamentally, each one has the same financial performance. What differs is how their business is funded.

Investors like Warren Buffet look at EBIT because they're more interested in the operating performance of a business, not how it was funded. This paints a clearer picture to understand the competitive advantage the company has compared to others.

Next time you refer to 'profit', make sure you're clear which one you're talking about.

The Three Levers to Improving Your Profit

Let's look at your P&L again. Notice how it's split into three distinct categories? That is, Revenue, Direct Costs and Operating Expenses.

Profit & Loss
Moo Formula Inc.
For the year ended 31 December 2017

	31-Dec-2017	
Revenue	$4,374,631	SALES LEVER
Direct Costs	$3,062,242	DIRECT COSTS LEVER
Gross Profit	$1,312,389	
Less Operating Expenses	$2,137,000	OPERATING COSTS LEVER
Net Profit	($824,611)	

Think of these as the levers to your company's profitability. For our purposes here, we'll label them as follows: the Sales Lever, Direct Costs Lever, and the Operating Expenses Lever.

LEVER 1 – THE SALES LEVER

The Sales Lever is the top line: revenue. It can be pulled either by increasing prices or increasing volume (selling more stuff).

LEVER 2 – THE DIRECT COSTS LEVER

Direct costs are all the fixed and variable expenses which can be directly attributed to the production of your product and service.

LEVER 3 – THE OPERATING EXPENSES LEVER

These are the fixed expenses—overhead like wages, utilities, and insurance—that you incur, irrespective of your revenue volume. Remember rent stays the same when sales go down. You might also hear them called SG&A (Sales, General and Administrative Costs).

These three levers form the profit controls to your machine. Within the levers, there are several moving pieces to coordinate— your product and service, wages, sales and marketing costs, and other expenses. The sum of these parts equate to the respective levers on your Profit & Loss statement.

The art to building your profitability machine is ensuring that these parts are all operating in sync, or as they say, 'well oiled'.

Allocating Your Costs to the Right Levers

The greatest challenge that I see with businesses trying to understand their gross profit is that it can be greatly affected by how the accounting is done. When undertaking the exercise of understanding your gross profit, it's crucially important that your bookkeeper and accountant are consistent with what costs should be allocated to direct costs versus other costs.

Most of these decisions are easy. In an inventory-based business, we know with certainty that the costs of the product and shipping should be allocated to Direct Costs.

Equally, there are plenty of expenses which are definitely considered Operating Costs, such as rent and office supplies.

But, there are also costs which sit in a grey area. For example, what about the wages of the employees that are in charge of logistics? Should these be classified as Direct Costs, since it's a cost of delivering the product? Or is it an Operating Cost, because that's where wages and salaries are allocated to?

In a service-based business, all the costs for your staff that are delivering and servicing your customers should be allocated to Direct Costs. That's because they are a direct cost of making your sales. If you didn't have your staff, you wouldn't have customers. However, it's rare that this actually happens in practice. Total wages are often allocated as a lump sum to Operating Costs.

MY RECOMMENDATION

Below is an example of how a detailed Profit & Loss should be structured.

Profit & Loss
Moo Formula Inc.
For the year ended 31 December 2017

	31-Dec-2017
REVENUE	$4,374,631
DIRECT COSTS	
Opening Stock	$1,000,000
Purchases	$3,012,242
Closing Stock	($1,500,000)
Wages - direct costs	$550,000
Total Direct Costs	$3,062,242
Gross Profit	$1,312,389
LESS OPERATING EXPENSES	
Customer Acquisition Costs	
Advertising and Marketing	$1,270,000
Wages - customer acquisition	$500,000
Total Customer Acquisition Costs	$1,770,000
General Expenses	
Rent	$150,000
Utilities	$47,000
Office Expenses	$20,000
Wages - general operations	$150,000
Total General Expenses	$367,000
Total Operating Expenses	$2,137,000
Net Profit	($824,611)

Here are a few suggestions as to how I use financial statements for decision making:

- Allocate all the wages costs related to servicing your clients and producing the work to 'Direct Costs'.

- Allocate all the wages costs for your sales and marketing staff under a cost bucket called 'Customer Acquisition Costs' as a sub-category under Operating expenses.

- Allocate all the wages for your management team, admin, and everything that doesn't fit into the previous two under a 'General Operations' cost bucket under Operating Costs.

Customer Acquisition Costs and General Operations are placed under the third lever, Operating Costs, which we'll explore soon.

WHY BOTHER WITH ALLOCATING WAGES?

When trying to understand how to drive profitability growth, splitting the employee expenses by function allows us to better understand profit margins, and also if we are efficiently acquiring new customers.

This gives us more accurate and meaningful data to further understand how we can improve the financial position. If everything is lumped together, it doesn't help us make decisions.

HOW TO PRACTICALLY SPLIT WAGE COSTS ACROSS FUNCTIONS

Here's a quick guide on wage allocations:

Employee Function	Cost Allocation
Management	Operating Costs - general operations
Sales and Marketing	Operating Costs - client acquisition costs
Revenue Generating	Direct Costs
Logistics	Direct Costs
Customer Success	Operating Costs - client acquisition costs
Product Development	Operating Costs - general operations
Operations	Operating Costs - general operations

I don't suggest you get too detailed and scientific with your approach on splitting the wages by function. Just allocate their wages by their role in the business.

If your employees keep timesheets, which I recommend for high-touch business models (see Principle 4) you can do it based on this. But again, keep it simple.

Now that you've got an understanding of the three profit levers, let's tinker with them.

"To every action there is always opposed an equal reaction."

Isaac Newton

MAXIMIZING YOUR LEVERS

Demystifying 'Cost Cutting'

When asked how to improve a company's profitability, the default response by your typical robot accountant is to "restructure your costs"—that is, slash your overhead expenses and fire staff. The list goes on like that: replace the espresso machine with instant coffee, or cancel the annual staff Christmas party. Sound familiar?

The problem I have with this advice is that it's wrong. Cutting petty expenses is not a sure way to improve profitability. In fact, it can have the reverse effect. When typical accountants and CFOs undertake 'cost cutting' exercises they only consider numbers on a Profit & Loss. What they often don't consider is the non-financial consequences of being a scrooge.

Trust me, I would know—I used to work for a huge, reputable accounting firm right as the Financial Crisis of 2008 hit the world's markets. In an effort to protect their profits, the partners of the firm undertook an 'efficiency exercise' known as Operation Tight-Ass.

They implemented petty policies like keeping a register of office stationery to prevent the 'excessive use' of pens. At one point, they even resorted to a BYO milk policy for the staff kitchen. Yes, it was a sad day for everyone.

The reason why I remember these trivial policies is because I experienced first-hand how it negatively impacted staff morale. The once high-performing culture was decimated overnight. It turned the managers into anal, petty subordinates and created an overall toxic work environment.

The irony was that this noble (but misguided) effort to reduce expenses actually had the reverse effect. The lost productivity, staff churn, and costs to administer these stupid policies ended up costing the firm more money. And for what? A few thousand bucks saved on milk every year?

My suggestions have nothing to do with slashing petty costs. I'm not interested in the small stuff. I care about making changes to only the most impactful financial levers in your business. The levers that, over time, can have massive results to your bottom line.

Maximizing Profit Leverage

The fun thing about your machine's three financial levers is they are not created equal. In other words, tinkering with them individually does not have an equal impact to profit. Simply focusing on a handful of techniques can do 80% of the heavy lifting.

Let's play with Moo Formula's levers to demonstrate my point.

PULLING THE SALES LEVER

We can pull the Sales Lever in two ways: increasing prices and increasing volume. Let's see the impact of this on Moo Formula's year end Profit & Loss statement on the next page.

First, let's yank on the lever by raising prices 10% on every item they sell. Since the direct costs and the operating expenses stay exactly the same, the benefit goes straight to net profit. In fact, there's a whopping 53% improvement over the base case.

Now, let's pull on the sales lever again, but this time increase volume by 10% (prices stay the same, but more stuff moves out the door). Hmm. Not as good. The net profit improvement is only 16%.

Profit & Loss
Moo Formula Inc.
For the year ended 31 December 2017

	Base Case	Sales Lever Price + 10%	Sales Lever Volume + 10%
Revenue	$4,374,631	$4,812,094	$4,812,094
Direct Costs	$3,062,242	$3,062,242	$3,368,466
Gross Profit	$1,312,389	$1,749,852	$1,443,628
Less Operating Expenses	$2,137,000	$2,137,000	$2,137,000
Net Profit	($824,611)	($387,148)	($693,372)
Net Profit Improvement		$437,463	$131,239
By Percentage		53 %	16 %

PULLING THE COSTS LEVER

So that's one way to impact profit: by bringing more money in. What about spending less money to begin with? Let's review the impact of playing with the Direct Cost and Operating Levers.

In the example on the next page, we start with the same base case as before. In the first attempt, we will reduce Direct Costs by 10%. Direct Costs are typically variable expenses. We can reduce them by producing our product or service more efficiently, or reducing the prices we pay to purchase them in the first place. In this example, reducing direct costs by 10% has a 37% improvement to profit. That's a whole lot of benefit without having to 'sell more'.

And what happens if we play with Operating Costs? Remember, Operating Cost are all your overheads like rent, utilities… and coffee. These costs are fixed in nature, which means they are not impacted by your revenue. In this example, reducing Operating Costs by 10% increases profit by 26%.

Profit & Loss
Moo Formula Inc.
For the year ended 31 December 2017

	Base Case	Direct Costs Lever (-10%)	Operating Lever (-10%)
Revenue	$4,374,631	$4,374,631	$4,374,631
Direct Costs	$3,062,242	$2,756,018	$3,062,242
Gross Profit	$1,312,389	$1,618,614	$1,312,389
Less Operating Expenses	$2,137,000	$2,137,000	$1,923,300
Net Profit	($824,611)	($518,386)	($610,911)
Net Profit Improvement		$306,225	$213,700
By Percentage		37 %	26 %

So, what's the best lever to pull? I've summarized the results below, in order of their effectiveness:

Financial Lever (10% change)	Profit Impact
Sales Lever - Price Increase	53 %
Direct Costs - Value Decrease	37 %
Operating Cost - Value Decrease	26 %
Sales Lever - Volume Increase	16 %

Do you see what I mean? The levers are not created equal.

When exploring tactics to improve your profitability, you should direct your focus to tinkering with the levers which have the greatest overall impact. When you have done all you can by tinkering with the first lever, move on to the next one. And so on.

Notice how the least impactful profit maximizing lever you can pull is to simply increase sales volume? Remember: Sales don't fix everything. Gross profit dollars do.

Now, let's dive into some tactics to improve your profits.

"Believe me, my journey has not been a simple journey of progress. There have been many ups and downs, and it is the choices that I made at each of those times that have helped shape what I have acheived."

Satya Nadella

PROFIT TACTICS FOR HIGH-TOUCH BUSINESSES

How Do You Peel a Banana?

That's easy. From the top, right? You pull the handle-like stem down to reveal the fruit. Hopefully, it's a ripe banana, or else you risk snapping the stem or squashing it. It's weird to explain, but I think you know what I'm talking about.

It turns out that humans have been peeling bananas all wrong. Monkeys peel bananas from the bottom. The process is simple: Flip the banana upside down, pinch the bottom until the peel splits, and then you're ready to remove it. It's way simpler and works every time. Try it next time.

Anyway, the profit-improving tips for high-touch companies in this chapter may challenge your accepted view of business. In other words, looking at it upside down might reveal a better way of doing things.

Profit Tactic #1: Cull Your Customers

To grow your revenue, you need to cull customers.

I know what you're thinking: Didn't you just say I need to grow revenue, not kill it off? Firing customers has the opposite effect!

Indeed, it sounds counter-intuitive to fire customers in order to grow revenue and profitability.

But, to move forward, you need to start by getting your house in order.

Customers are Killing Your Business

In the early days of starting up my company, I had no idea what I was doing. Okay, I knew how to do the technical work, but I had no idea of what my 'ideal customer' looked like. Accordingly, when it came to engaging new clients, I wasn't fussy. I didn't care who they were, as long as they paid me. I was focused on sales.

The challenge with business—particularly in the early phases of a new venture—is that it's very difficult to say 'no'. You take every meeting, every phone call, every bit of work that comes your way.

Even if you know in your heart and on paper that you might just break-even or even lose money on a customer or project, you'll say 'yes'. Because, you never know, it may lead to something bigger.

My newly formed habit of being a 'yes man' proved to be completely flawed as my business grew rapidly, from a revenue perspective anyway. Although sales were growing, we were losing money. Profit margins were getting squeezed due to my habit of 'discounting' to win work.

Furthermore, due to misaligned client expectations, service declined. Customers were getting frustrated and were churning. As a result, I was losing more customers than I won. My financial and mental health was suffering as a result.

I was slaving away—14 hours a day, 7 days a week, feeling over-whelmed and too busy to realize what I was doing wrong.

I mean, it could have been okay if I was profitable, but the truth was that I wasn't. From a revenue perspective, I was crushing it. My business was consistently doing 20% month-on-month revenue growth (which is impressive growth for any business, irrespective of industry or size). The problem, however, was while the top-line revenue was growing, I was actually losing money. I was servicing unprofitable customers. I hadn't designed a process to service our customers consistently, and profitably.

I was stuck in a profit-losing machine of my own design— relentlessly spinning cogs.

I was trapped.

How to Do a Customer Analysis

With the business spiralling out of control, something had to change. My partner and I spent a Sunday afternoon to take time away from the company and objectively analyze it. It was time to wear our 'business owner' hat and assess our financial performance.

What we unearthed validated our 'gut feel' assumption: our company was a disaster.

The irony was that, while we were supposed to be helping our customers with their firm's financial performance, I couldn't even do it myself.

"How ironic," I thought to myself. I felt like an imposter.

"Here we go again…"

Quickly snapping myself out of an emotional state, my rational brain got to work: starting with a customer profitability analysis.

In our analysis, we discovered that the profit generated by the top 20% of our customers absorbed the losses of the bottom 80%!

In other words, we were suffering because we were not selective about our ideal customers.

Being a 'yes' person was killing our business.

Chances are, it's also killing yours.

Here's a step-by-step guide of how we undertook our customer analysis.

STEP 1 – EXPORT A SALES REPORT

Export a sales report from your accounting system to a spreadsheet. Filter this data by customer name and rank by $ value of sales for the last 12-month period.

STEP 2 – ASK QUESTIONS

For each customer ask yourself the following questions.

1.   Are they easy to work with?
2.   Do they pay their bills on time?
3.   Are they a brand ambassador/influencer for what you sell?
4.   Do I like them as people?

For questions 1, 2 and 3, assign a score out 0 to 3 (0 being terrible, 3 being amazing).

For the fourth and final question, make that one binary. It's a 0 or 1.

Tally your results, which will give you a qualitative score out of 10 for each customer.

Here's an example:

Qualitative Criteria	Score
Are they easy to work with?	2
Do they pay their bills on time?	3
Are they a brand ambassador/influencer?	1
Do you like them as people?	0
TOTAL	6/10

The process of allocating a score against each question helps you to assess your customers objectively. This quantification serves to eliminate any biases you have towards your customers.

STEP 3 – CALCULATE THE DIRECT COST

Calculate the average direct cost to service each customer and enter the value in a new column. You can allocate this off your timesheet data or project management system (see Principle 4).

STEP 4 – CALCULATE THE GROSS PROFIT

Calculate the gross profit earned on each customer by deducting the average costs to service each customer from the sales dollars.

STEP 5 – SORT YOUR CUSTOMERS BY GROSS PROFIT

Filter the spreadsheet by gross profit of each customer and rank them per Step 2. The result is a list of your most profitable, desirable customers. They're the ones you want to clone (see Profit Tactic #2). And, at the bottom of the list, are the ones you want to cull.

Income by Contact
Voltage Media LLC
For the 12 months ended 31 December 2017

Customer	Total Sales	Customer Score	Cost to Service	Gross Profit per Client
Tezla	$10,000	6	$35,000	($25,000)
Hoolio	$15,000	4	$40,000	($25,000)
Pied Piper	$40,000	4	$55,000	($15,000)
Facelook	$12,500	4	$17,000	($4,500)
Tencents	$12,500	4	$17,000	($4,500)
Orange Inc.	$36,000	2	$40,000	($4,000)
SaaSy	$225,000	8	$228,000	($3,000)
Berk Hazway	$42,000	5	$40,000	$2,000
Purple Cow	$40,000	5	$35,000	$5,000
Giggle	$400,000	8	$283,000	$117,000
Amazing	$317,000	6	$100,000	$217,000
Macrosoft	$350,000	7	$60,000	$290,000
Herizon	$900,000	9	$400,000	$500,000
TOTAL	$2,400,000		$1,350,000	$1,050,000

The table above is a sample customer profitability analysis for Voltage Media. Here are the key observations.

1. The customers under Note 1 are the ones Brendan should sack. They rank low on the qualitative Customer Score, and they are loss making.

2. The customer SaaSy under Note 2 is not so obvious. They bring in a lot of revenue, and have a high customer score. However, they're being serviced unprofitably. In these situations, Brendan should dig deeper to understand why this client is unprofitable. Perhaps it's because he's over-servicing them or not producing their work efficiently?

3. The customers under Note 3 are fence-sitters. They rank in the middle from a customer perspective, and they generate a small profit to Brendan's business. It's okay for Brendan to hang-on to these customers, but he should monitor them.

4. These customers rank highly on the customer score, and they bring in the most profit to the business. Notice how the profit generated from these clients carry the losses of the bottom half? These are the customers to clone.

How to Sack Your Customers

In the 24 hours that followed our customer analysis, I made several simple, but emotionally difficult decisions that literally changed my business. I took steps to fire the unprofitable 80% of my customers.

My outreach email exchange was something like this:

Subj: Price Changes

Hey Customer,

I'm reaching out to inform you of a few internal changes at our company. We've spent the last 12 months servicing our customers of all shapes and sizes, from startups to larger businesses. To date, we've been flexible to cater for all these different businesses as we want to help as many businesses as possible. As you can appreciate, being tailored for everyone does come at a cost.

After reviewing our service offering and the associated fees, we are changing our prices. Your account will fall into the new package at $XX per month. This investment will ensure we're able to continue to maintain our level of service.

Please reach out if you have any thoughts on the above. If I don't hear from you in the next 10 days we'll assume you're comfortable with the new arrangement.

Subj: RE: Price Changes
Dear Jason,
I must say it is not an appealing proposition at all. As we have always been dealing with you, we fail to see what is different now and, more surprisingly, how it can double the monthly cost of the service you provide to us.

Subj: RE: RE: Price Changes
Hey Customer,
I agree nothing has changed since engaging us, however our recent review showed we cannot service you profitably at the current rates. I hope you appreciate this doesn't make business sense for us. I can refer you to a cheaper alternative if you wish. Let me know and I can make the introduction.

As expected, a handful of customers left us and were happy to accept our referral recommendation to another service provider. What we didn't expect was that the majority of customers accepted the price increases, and continue to be our customers today.

Giving your customers clear options to either pay a higher rate, or be referred to a cheaper alternative makes the decision binary, leaving no room for time-wasting negotiations. Make the decision easy for your customers. They are busy people as well.

The net result was that we actually increased revenue because the price increase offset the churned, unprofitable clients! Making the decision to cull these bad customers built a new platform capable of efficient and sustainable longer-term growth. Although we had fewer customers, we were more profitable at a gross profit level; had more time; and were, most importantly, less stressed.

And that leads us to our next tactic.

Profit Tactic #2: Cloning Your Best Customers

A customer analysis will not only help you identify the customers to fire—it also helps you identify your best ones. Picture your perfect client. The one that never challenges your fees. The one that always pays on time. The one that trusts your work. Now, imagine landing 100 clones of that exact customer. Wouldn't that put you in a position to run a happier and financially healthier business?

Having customers with similar needs and behaviors offers a number of profit-maximizing benefits, including:

- **Efficiency of Service**
  Building products and services around a specific customer provides efficiency gains as a result of repeatability and consistency, rather than varying needs.

- **Targeted Marketing**
  An intimate knowledge of your best customers allows you to narrow your marketing towards a specific channel, resulting in cheaper customer acquisition costs (see the next chapter).

- **Own the Market**
  You know that feeling when a brand just seems to know you? Try to own your space and dominate a niche. Word of mouth is the best form of marketing.

Characterize Your Best Customers

After reviewing our bottom 80% of customers, we took the customer analysis exercise a step further by deep diving into the characteristics of our best customers. These included:

- Business model/Industry
- Demographics of the founder
- Geography
- Revenue
- Number of employees

We discovered that all of our best customers had common characteristics. For us, it was apparent that the industry, revenue, and demographics of the founder were the common attributes. We knew this by gut feel, but it was validated with numbers. Knowing our ideal customers allowed us to focus our efforts on nurturing them and exploring where to find more of them.

Ultimately, the customer analysis process helped us to define our target market, and set us up to narrow our focus on acquiring more of them.

Profit Tactic #3: Optimize Your Productivity

By far one of the biggest financial performance issues I see in labor-intensive businesses, such as services, is under-utilization of staff.

In a company where value is created as a direct result of a person's output—like law-firms and marketing agencies—we can compare the amount of time spent on creating value for clients versus the total time spent working in the business.

For example, if an employee is at work for 8 hours a day and spends 4 hours creating value for a client; 2 hours in internal meetings; and 2 hours on lunch, coffees, and chatting with friends, then that person would be considered 50% utilized.

Of course, the more productive an employee is, the more revenue will be generated. At a more complex level it could be said that the 2 hours spent in internal meetings from the above example was necessary for running the business.

The general point is that a business owner wants employees to be as productive as possible.

I've included a variety of techniques and tactics to improve employee utilization in Principle 4: Leverage Your Assets.

Employees are your greatest asset after all.

"A journey of a thousand miles begins with a single step."

Lao-Tzu

PROFIT TACTICS FOR LOW-TOUCH BUSINESSES

Let's Get Down and Dirty

Hey, you're a low-touch business? Cool. These profit-improving tactics are for you. In this chapter, I've detailed the three primary tactics that businesses like yours need to maximize profit margins. Some of them might be obvious. Some maybe not. What they all have in common is the need to get your hands dirty in the data.

Profit Tactic #4: Know Your Product Mix

When you walk down the pharmaceuticals aisle of your local grocery store, which toothpaste do you buy?

Perhaps you're a caffeine junkie, so you opt for the Advanced Teeth Whitening formula. Or, maybe your spouse commented on your bad breath, so you choose Triple Action. Or, perhaps, it's the family-friendly Spider-Man Gel to keep the kids happy?

Colgate has over 30 toothpaste products, all designed for a particular consumer in mind. Yes, the branding is different and the ingredients vary slightly. But, fundamentally, toothpaste is just toothpaste, right?

You could say the same for pain killers.

In 2015, Nurofen, one of Australia's leading ibuprofen brands was investigated by the Australian Competition and Consumer and Commission (ACCC) for misleading conduct. The company was in trouble for falsely advertising its new 'Specific Pain Products'—a line of products marketed as pain relief for specific types of pain ranging from back pain, to period pain, to migraines.

This would have been okay if it were true, but it wasn't. The underlying products were the same. Identical mix of ingredients, identical manufacturing processes—identical everything.

Corporations spend billions of dollars every year developing products to meet the needs of different market segments. They even risk breaking the law to do it.

New is Cool

In the consumable goods land where commoditization is rampant, the key to separating yourself from the pack is branding. Creating a variety of tailored and customized products to serve different customers is one tactic to differentiate yourself from competitors.

From an outsider's perspective, having a range of products is great for sales. The more market segments you can dominate, the greater total market share you can take. This translates to more sales, right?

The challenge is that differentiation through customization comes at a cost. With the focus on sales and brand positioning, it's easy to ignore the impact of the costs to produce and manufacture these various products.

The incentive for sales and marketing managers to increase market share from new products often conflicts with the financial priorities of the business. Having a broad range of products is great for sales, but you still need to make money from them.

The art is ensuring you are meeting the ever-evolving shifts in consumer expectations, while still being able to optimize the sales mix of these products and the overall gross profit.

This is the dark art known as your Product Mix.

Product Mix Versus Profit Margin

If you're like most low-touch businesses, you will have a range of products to sell. These products often require different resources, both in time and cost to produce. Accordingly, your products will have varying gross profits.

Product mix is the term used to describe the combination of these products sold to your customers.

Let's look at our e-commerce business example, Moo Formula. They're a baby formula retailer with 3 products. The details of each product are listed below, ranked by the sales price per product.

Product List
Moo Formula Inc.

Product	Retail Price	Cost to make	Profit per SKU	Profit Margin
Premium Formula A+	$49.95	$37.00	$12.95	26 %
Bare Formula B+	$34.95	$15.00	$19.95	57 %
Eco Pacifier	$9.95	$3.00	$6.95	70 %

The company's flagship product Premium Formula A+ has the highest sales price at $49.95 per unit, but has the lowest gross profit margin at 26%.

The Bare Formula B+, the middle grade formula on the other hand has a lower sales price at $34.95 but a much higher gross profit margin at 57%.

The Eco Pacifier, a dummy, has the lowest sales price, but the highest profit margin.

Optimizing Your Product Mix

The dark art of blending marketing and finance is optimizing your product mix so you can maximize the overall gross profit of your company.

Let's look at the product mix of sales for December, 2017.

Product Mix Analysis - Dec 2017
Moo Formula Inc.

Product	Retail Price	# Units Sold	Gross Sales $	Gross Profit
Premium Formula A+	$49.95	5,150	$257,243	$66,692 (26%)
Bare Formula B+	$34.95	3,200	$111,840	$63,840 (57%)
Eco Pacifier	$9.95	1,650	$16,418	$11,468 (70%)
TOTAL		10,000	$385,500	$142,000 (37%)

Of the total 10,000 units sold in December, the overall gross profit percentage on total sales is 37%. This is because the Premium Formula, which has the lowest gross profit margin had the most units sold, which weighs down on the overall gross profit for the month. Now, let's tinker with the product mix.

Adjusted Product Mix - Dec 2017
Moo Formula Inc.

Product	Retail Price	# Units Sold	Gross Sales $	Gross Profit
Premium Formula A+	$49.95	4,150	$207,293	$53,743 (26%)
Bare Formula B+	$34.95	4,200	$146,790	$83,790 (57%)
Eco Pacifier	$9.95	1,650	$16,418	$11,4678 (70%)
TOTAL		10,000	$370,500	$149,000 (40%)
Net Benefit			($15,000)	$7,000 (3%)

In the example above, we reduced the quantity sold of Premium Formula A+ by 1,000 units, and instead sold 1,000 additional units of Bare Formula B+. However, the total amount sold of all products remained at 10,000 units.

The net result was that sales dollars reduced, but the overall gross profit increased by 3%. This is because the company sold more units of product that have a higher gross profit margin.

Of course, improving the overall unit sales would have helped even more, but this example shows the power of tinkering with your product mix and how it can impact overall profitability.

Simply put, if you're working within a constraint of sales volume and want to increase gross profit, consider adjusting the mix of sales to your customers.

What if You Have Low-Margin Products?

Gary Vaynerchuck (or Vee) is an entrepreneur, internet celebrity, and founder of Wine Library and VaynerMedia. Gary Vee is best known for leveraging digital marketing platforms to scale his parent's liquor store business from $3M sales to $60M in sales.

From a vanity metric perspective, this sounds great. But, as we've learned, sales are only one part of the equation.

In episode 89 of *The Gary Vee Show*, he gives an insight into the financials behind his parent's liquor business. Liquor stores have notoriously low gross profit margins—with products as low as 10%.

"The liquor business is bad because there's a middle wholesale part that takes 25% of the 50% that a retailer normally takes."

Gary shares a tactic he used to transform low-margin products from a defensive posture to an offensive one. Low-margin products generally have brand equity, so he used them to lure customers into his store. Once his customers were in 'buying mode', he used that opportunity to upsell them—offering higher-margin products.

In my opinion, having high gross profit margins is the best strategy. You should be investing your resources and time into developing new products with higher margins. But, if you are working within a constraint, consider using low-margin products as lures to upsell your customers into high-margin products.

Know Your Margins

As the founder and CEO, it's critically important for you to have an intimate understanding of your product mix. I can't stress enough how much you need to know each product's gross profit.

The costs attributable to your products isn't just subject to the raw materials either. You should be factoring 'fully landed costs'. Fully landed cost is the total price of a product once it has arrived at a buyer's door—which includes price of the product, taxes, all transportation fees, customs, duties, insurance, and currency conversion.

It sounds like a mouthful, and it can be painful from an accounting perspective. But there are a range of tools to help you accurately account for them.

An IMS is Your Best Friend

An Inventory Management System (IMS) can assist you with accurately recording and attributing direct costs to your various product lines. Not only does it give you visibility over your product mix, but it can also help you forecast re-order points and inform overall efficiency of your operations.

Inventory Management Systems used to be reserved for big retailers and corporates. But cloud software has democratized the game. There are a number of cloud-based tools available for small and growing businesses that integrate into accounting and sales platforms. To head you in the right direction, I've included a list of inventory management systems at the end of this Principle.

In summary, if you're running a product-based business and want to improve your bottom line, start by getting an intimate understanding of your product mix. Explore tweaking and optimizing your mix so you can maximize sales and margins.

Profit Tactic #5: 1% Improvements to Your Sales Funnel

Okay, I am not—and don't claim to be—a customer acquisition mastermind. I will not offer a Facebook marketing hack to instantly 10x your sales, so you can become an instant millionaire (we'll leave that for gurus like Tai Lopez).

I am, however, acutely aware of the parts and numbers to your sales machine that drive your revenue. Managing and measuring everything is the first step to improving the predictability of your sales. It starts with getting granular with your sales funnel.

The revenue equation is this:

$$LEADS \times CONVERSION\ RATE \times AVG.\ SALE\ PRICE = REVENUE$$

Break down your sales funnel data from your CRM and pay attention to your 'conversion rate'. Making marginal gains to your conversion rate can provide massive results to revenue. Let's take a look at Moo Formula again.

Sales Funnel
Moo Formula Inc.

	Base	1% Improvement
# of Monthly Visitors	30,000	30,000
% Conversion Rate	18%	19%
$ Average Sale Price	$75	$75
Revenue Per Month	$405,000	$427,500
Net Revenue Gain		$22,500
By Percentage		6 %

In the example above, just a 1% improvement to the conversion rate on website traffic resulted in a 6% revenue growth per month.

The bottom line? Fix the holes in your leaky conversion bucket before simply adding more leads. Test everything.

Generating New Leads

Building a sales and marketing engine to generate predictable leads is often considered the greatest challenge of any business. Markets and people are irrational, and finding your target customer—and hitting them when they're ready to buy—can be expensive. It may cost you more than that customer generates in sales.

The art to building a profitable growth engine is understanding how much you should spend to acquire these new customers. We'll get to this shortly.

For a more predictable—and often shorter sales cycle—I prefer to focus attention and marketing dollars on upselling products to existing customers. Customers that have already established trust with your brand tend to have a higher conversion rate as well.

Would You Like Fries with That?

Humans are impulsive, irrational creatures. When we say we'll wake up early and go to the gym, we sleep in. We say we should diet, yet end up buying chocolate at the gas station. We default to the most primitive part of our brain to make emotive decisions.

Smart companies like McDonalds manipulate our lizard brain, going for the upsell when we're most vulnerable—the moment is when we're in 'buying mode' with a juicy Big Mac on our mind. Identifying and capitalizing on these buying modes is the key to generating incremental upsells, and profits.

Consider your customer's buying modes and opportunities for upsells. It could be as simple as asking, "Would you like fries with that?"

Profit Tactic #6: Hack Your Customer Aquisition Costs

In high-growth businesses, customer acquisition costs—that is, all costs incurred in relation to finding and selling to new customers—is the most expensive and challenging aspect of cost management. Founders often only look at sales growth as a metric to understand if their customer acquisition is effective.

The problem with that is they don't often consider the efficiency of their sales machine. If you don't have a true understanding of your customer acquisition costs, the risk is that you spend more money acquiring customers than they are worth to you. The net result is a loss with no financial benefit.

How Much Should I Spend on Sales and Marketing?

We hear the stories of startups raising bucket loads of capital and burning it all very quickly. Uber, WeWork, Snapchat—all are raising cash to increase their market share and build a competitive advantage around their business, so they can't be disrupted.

Inevitably, the financial situations of companies like these look pretty dire. They're losing money and eating up all their cash. Accordingly, analyzing these companies from the lens of traditional financial measures like profit is futile. They have no profit!

Investors and VCs, who would normally assess a business on traditional financial indicators and metrics, need to look outside the realm of P&Ls and Balance Sheets to understand if these companies are worthy of their money.

So what do they look at?

In assessing the viability of low-touch business models, there are two metrics investors consider. The first metric is understanding the lifetime value of a customer. The second metric is the cost of customer acquisition. Let's start with the latter.

Customer Acquisition Costs (CAC) are all expenses incurred in acquiring/winning new customers. These include:

- Wages for your sales and marketing team
- Digital advertising expenses like Google Adwords
- Expenses for events and trade shows
- Any other expenses to do with onboarding new customers

In order to understand the total cost you incur to acquire a customer, you calculate the unit cost by dividing the total expense over the number of new customers.

CUSTOMER ACQUISTION COSTS =
CUSTOMER ACQUISITION COSTS / # OF NEW CUSTOMERS

The formula calculates a 'per unit cost' of acquiring a customer over a period. Typically this is on a monthly or quarterly basis.

Let's look at an example.

In the quarter ended December 31, 2017, Moo Formula spent $100,000 on customer acquisition expenses in the form of:

- Facebook marketing: $50,000
- Google Adwords: $35,000
- Trade Show: $15,000

The total number of new customers acquired from those marketing efforts was 500.

Customer Acquisition Cost Analysis
Moo Formula Inc.
For the quarter ended 31 December 2017

	Marketing Spend	# New Customers
Facebook Advertising	$50,000	100
Google Adwords	$35,000	250
Tradeshows	$15,000	150
	$100,000	500

Average Customer Acqusition Cost	$200

On average, Moo Formula spends $200 to acquire every new customer.

Measuring CAC is a crucial metric as it helps business owners understand the profitability of marketing and sales efforts.

If you have multiple channels of acquiring new customers, measuring CAC can help you objectively ascertain which channel is the most profitable for your business. This data can help you assess whether you should:

- Double down on the most efficient channel, and/or
- Improve the less profitable ones, or scrap them altogether

You can do this by further breaking down the marketing channels you have in your business to acquire new customers.

Customer Acquisition Cost Analysis
Moo Formula Inc.
For the quarter ended 31 December 2017

	Marketing Spend	# New Customers	CAC per Channel
Facebook Advertising	$50,000	100	$500
Google Adwords	$35,000	250	$140
Tradeshows	$15,000	150	$100
TOTAL	$100,000	500	

By doing some analysis, we can see that 'Tradeshows' are the most efficient Customer Acquisition Channel, with a unit CAC of $100 per customer. The least efficient channel is Facebook advertising, with a unit CAC of $500 per customer. Sarah should research why trade shows have been her most efficient means of gaining new customers. Also, she should think about redirecting the money spent on Facebook marketing to trade shows instead.

Managing all costs incurred for finding and selling to new customers is often the most expensive and challenging aspect of cost management for low-touch business models. Having an acute understanding if you're 'over spending on CAC' is therefore critical.

So how do you know if you're overspending?

It all depends on how much a customer is worth to you. We can determine this by calculating your Customer Lifetime Value.

Calculating the Value of a Customer

Customer Lifetime Value (CLV) is a fancy word to predict the future profit you will make over the entire relationship with a customer. It's a formula to help you quantify what a customer is worth to you in financial measures so you can understand if they are worth acquiring (via sales and marketing) in the first place.

The Customer Lifetime Value calculation can have varying levels of sophistication, ranging from 'gut feel' (low cost and rubbery) to the use of complex predictive analytics techniques (higher cost and still rubbery). For the sake of our friend Pareto, I'm going to run through the simple version of the formula.

$$CUSTOMER\ LIFETIME\ VALUE\ =\ ANNUAL\ GROSS\ PROFIT$$
$$PER\ CUSTOMER\ X\ AVERAGE\ NUMBER\ OF\ YEARS$$

Once more, let's look at Moo Formula as an example.

A loyal customer of Moo Formula has a monthly subscription to purchase the Premium B+ baby formula which retails at $34.95. This customer buys this particular formula once a month, so they will spend a total of $419.40 per annum. It's expected the customer will buy the formula for the next 2 years.

At a 57% gross profit margin, the customer is worth $239 of annual gross profit to Moo Formula.

Customer Lifetime Value = $239 * 2 years
Customer Lifetime Value = $478

Now that we know what a customer is worth to Moo Formula, we can delve into how much the company can spend on acquiring similar customers. We do this with the Customer Acquisition Cost to Customer Lifetime Value ratio.

Customer Lifetime Value to Customer Acquisition Cost

To understand if you are acquiring new customers profitability, let's take a deep dive into the relationship between CLV and CAC. This magic ratio helps you determine whether you are getting 'bang for your buck' on the money you spend acquiring new customers to your business.

The magic ratio is this:

$$CUSTOMER\ LIFETIME\ VALUE\ TO$$
$$CUSTOMER\ ACQUISITION\ COST\ RATIO\ =\ 3{:}1$$

Essentially, the value of your customers needs to be at least 3 times the value of what you spend to acquire them in the first place. If your ratio is less than this, the money out the door acquiring these customers basically outweighs any future profits that they might generate for you. This is bad.

Understanding your CLV:CAC ratio is therefore a great tool to help you to determine the upper limit of money you should budget with regards to sales and marketing expenses.

Let's look at two different scenarios to demonstrate my point.

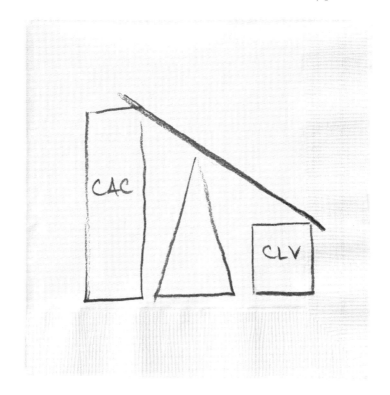

The napkin diagram (above) represents a business that's in trouble. You will see that the costs they are incurring to acquire new customers are higher than what the customer is ultimately worth to the business.

Sure, having lots of new customers means lots of new revenue. As business owners it's easy for us to get swept in the vanity metric of 'revenue growth'. (Trust me; I've been there, too.) We can get obsessive about pumping lots of money into paid advertising and sales teams, which should drive revenue growth.

The problem is this: if the overall costs to acquire these new customers outweigh any future potential profit that customer will bring to your business, you're essentially losing money on each one. You may have other reasons for the outreach, but—from a financial perspective—it's kind of pointless.

It's like buying friends to make you happy. Nobody wants that.

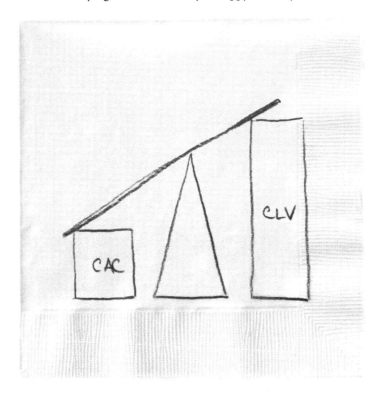

Portrayed on the napkin above is better example to follow. Here the CAC is significantly less than the CLV.

A strong business model is one that efficiently acquires valuable customers. The value of a new customer is multiple times higher than the cost of acquiring them in the first place.

So maybe you're asking: What's the sweet spot? In other words, how many more times does the expected value of new customers need to be compared to the costs of acquiring them?

The sweet spot to target is at least three-to-one (3:1). That is, the value of the customers you are acquiring should be at least 3 times the cost of acquiring them in the first place. If you're acquiring customers at this rate, you should be happy.

If your CLV:CAC ratio is one-to-one (1:1), as a new business, you're losing money. This means the costs to acquire new customers outweigh the future value they will bring to your business.

If your ratio is around 2:1, that means you are only breaking even on every new customer.

Let's look at Moo Formula again to see a practical example.

Customer Acquisition Cost Analysis
Moo Formula Inc.
For the quarter ended 31 December 2017

	Marketing Spend	CAC per Channel	CLV:CAC Ratio
Facebook Advertising	$50,000	$500	1.0 x
Google Adwords	$35,000	$140	3.4 x
Tradeshows	$15,000	$100	4.8 x
TOTAL	$100,000		

Examining the ratios, it's obvious that Sarah's most profitable acquisition channels are Google Adwords and 'Tradeshows'. Her Facebook initiative, however, is actually losing money.

I'd suggest that she consider scrapping her Facebook advertising as it's not generating a financial return to the business.

What If my Customer Acquisition Costs are Too High?

If you're not acquiring customers efficiently, the question you need to ask is: How do you lower the costs? I have two tactics to suggest.

TACTIC 1 – ANALYZE YOUR CUSTOMER ACQUISITION CHANNELS

Interrogate your customer acquisition cost data so you can understand the cost of each channel. This helps you to decide whether to double down on a more effective channel, or scrap the poor performing ones altogether.

TACTIC 2 – FOCUS ON CUSTOMER SUCCESS

The other method, which I find is relatively under-utilized by most businesses, is having 'customer success' personnel.

This should be a role at your company—a person, or team, responsible for managing the customer relationship. The position is typically focused on long-term value generation for the customer.

By having a great customer success team, you ensure your current customers are so happy that they're loyal to your brand, buy more products from you, and even refer more customers. All of these increase customer lifetime value and lower customer acquisition costs through free, word-of-mouth marketing.

Trust the Process

Early in my teens, I was the overweight, dorky computer game nerd. I had a growing *Warhammer 40k* army, and was the proud owner of a obsessively-complete Pokemon card collection.

I also enjoyed cooking. Actually, I preferred the eating part over the cooking.

My younger brother and I spent our weekends experimenting with different recipes in the family kitchen. From triple-cooked fried chicken and giant omelettes to stir-fries and casseroles. We scoured the internet for recipes and cooked everything our hearts desired.

If you spend your weekends mostly cooking and eating, your waistline will naturally grow. As the saying goes 'never trust a skinny cook'. Accordingly, I was the fat kid at school. I was chubby growing up and was always picked on and teased by the other kids because of my weight.

In my teenage years I was tired of being bullied, so I did something about it.

I remember my first ever 'gym session' at the age of 15. I spent 40 minutes on the treadmill. After working up a sweat, I stood in front of the mirror, expecting to see results. But I noticed nothing.

No change.

I was disheartened with the lack of progress. I went to the gym the following day and did the same routine. Again, no change. I thought, "Clearly, I'm not doing something right."

After several days not seeing any results, I became disheartened. The process of looking at myself in the mirror was killing my motivation. So I stopped doing it—looking in the mirror, that is. I still kept going to the gym.

It wasn't until after a few months of my new habit that people were commenting on my appearance. My love-handles were slowly disappearing. My arms were getting more toned. What validated the external feedback was the falling numbers on the scale. What I realized was that focusing on the process—not the outcome—was the key to keeping myself motivated.

My point is, nothing happens overnight. Like trying to shed a few pounds of fat, improving the profitability of your business is a process. There is no single 'event'. It's an accumulation of small tweaks and persistent effort which result in cumulative gains.

The craft for you, the operator, is an intimate understanding of your financial levers. Whatever actions you make, adopt a posture of experimentation. Test a hypothesis, measure the result, and learn from your experiments. Trust the process.

Take control of your machine, and make it work for you.

Principle 2 Takeaways

- In any business, there are three forms of profit to focus on: Gross Profit, Net Profit, and Operating Profit.

- Sales don't fix everything, gross profit dollars do. High gross profit margins are an indicator of efficiency. Before scaling your sales, ensure that you have optimized your gross profit margins.

- Operating Profit is a better reflection of your performance than Net Profit, because it's not skewed by taxes or interest expenses.

- There are three levers to profitability: the Sales Lever, the Direct Costs Lever, and the Operating Costs Lever. Correctly allocating your expenses and income to the levers in your Profit & Loss will help you understand how to pull them.

- However, the three Profit Levers are not created equal. The Direct Costs and Sales Levers are the most impactful ones. In fact, these two provide 80% of the impact on your profits.

PROFITABILITY TACTICS FOR HIGH-TOUCH BUSINESSES

- Bad customers are killing your business. A profitability analysis is a useful tool to understand which customers you should fire.

- Clone your best customers. A profitability analysis can also identify your best clients. Having customers with similar needs and behaviors offer a number of profit-maximizing benefits.

- Optimize your productivity. Staff is the biggest expense for the majority of businesses. The key to increasing profitability is to maximize the value they are creating on a daily basis.

PROFITABILITY TACTICS FOR LOW-TOUCH BUSINESSES

- Optimize your product mix. Every product has a different direct cost to produce. Understanding the gross profit for each offering helps you maximize the company's overall gross profit.

- Try to make incremental improvements to your sales funnel. Big changes start with small steps, no matter how small.

- Optimize your customer acquisition costs. If you don't, the risk is that you will spend more money acquiring customers than they are worth. Have a budget that informs your actions. We'll explore this concept more in Principle 5.

SOFTWARE TOOLS FOR PRINCIPLE 2

To help you reach your profitability goals, you might want to explore the following Inventory Management Systems:

- DEAR Systems: http://dearsystems.com/inventory-software/

- Unleashed: https://www.unleashedsoftware.com/

- Trade Gecko: https://www.tradegecko.com/

- Fishbowl Inventory: https://www.fishbowlinventory.com/

SUPER-CHARGE YOUR CASH FLOW

REVENUE IS BULLSHIT

Sorry, let me say that more gently. I think revenue is vanity. Profit is sanity. Cash is reality. This section teaches how to turn your business into a cash flow-generating machine.

"Revenue is vanity, profit is sanity, cash is reality."

A proverb by any entrepreneur trying to make payroll.

PROFIT IS NOT CASH

Is Profit Wrong?

Profit is perceived as a dirty word in business. The connotations around the term 'profit' are of selfishness, greed, and capitalism. We might think of balding, overweight executives smoking cigars in boardrooms, perched in 100-story ivory towers—looking down on us plebs doing the daily grind.

Moreover, we often hear emotive and grandiose declarations from corporate idols like Sir Richard Branson that 'business should be driven by purpose, not profit.' The well-off (who've already made their millions) implore us to make bold vision statements, to make the world a better place, to improve the lives of others. I agree.

A company should be guided with purpose, meaning, and aspiration. It shouldn't just be about printing stacks of money.

Can you imagine a firm saying, "Our mission is to be the world's most profitable company." Not exactly inspiring, right?

Don't get me wrong; while I think that putting purpose over profit is admirable, following this advice literally can be dire. The reality is that, without profit, your business is a charity. And it won't be around long. To create an enterprise that outlives its founders decades into the future, you need cash—cash from sales.

Sure, there are investors and financiers to help fund our vision, but this is not a long-term business strategy. They will want their money back eventually.

The best way to be self-sufficient is to generate your own cash flow. Cash flow, generated by profit.

Your CPA Defines Profit Differently

Now, before we continue, I want to clear something up. Despite my ramblings on why you should care so much about profit, I want you to understand that the 'profit' your CPA accountant reports to you annually isn't real. Allow me to explain.

On January 1st of every year, while the world is nursing hangovers and gorging on leftover Christmas ham, there is one group of people who are preparing for the greatest three months of their lives. They are nesting in their offices, stocking their Bic pens, and priming their calculators.

These odd creatures, of course, are the elusive and bespectacled CPAs. While you're setting New Year's resolutions, the CPAs are preparing themselves for the bountiful harvest of tax season—a three-month window where millions of small businesses flock to them in order to have their taxes filed with the IRS.

If you're reading this book, I'm going to assume you've had the pleasure of working with a CPA. I'll hazard a guess that your experience went a little something like this:

- In early January, Sandra your bookkeeper, scrambles to crunch your numbers for the last three months. After asking about the nature of your entertainment and travel expenses, she sends your Quickbooks file to Bob, your CPA.

- Bob the CPA calls you, out of the blue, firstly to ask about the weather, then acknowledges that he received your accounting files from Sandra. He gets to work and advises that your taxes will be completed in a month.

- Three months later, just days before the filing deadline, you finally get a phone call from Bob. He asks you to meet at his office to sign some paperwork.

- At the meeting, Bob hands you a shiny, bloated, meaningless report for your review. He directs your attention to the 'profit' and congratulates you on having a 'good year'.

- He then presents another report showing the reconciliation of that accounting profit to your taxable profit, then how much tax you have to pay on that taxable profit.

- You sit there, dazed and confused, trying to digest what the hell is going on. Bob continues to ramble on about changes to the tax law this year and his plans to buy a new Mercedes.

- On the drive back to the office, your mind races—trying to comprehend what Bob presented to you. You wonder why all that profit isn't actually cash in your bank account, and also: How the hell you are going to pay that tax bill?

- After a few hours of trying to understand the tax result, you give up and place it in the 'too hard basket'. After all, you trust Bob and his decades of experience. But, at least, the ordeal is over for another year. You write a check for the tax bill, and cross your fingers that it doesn't bounce.

Does this sound familiar?

Of course, I am stereotyping. Not all CPAs are like Bob. Most drive Volvos instead.

You Can't Pay Bills With Profit

Jokes aside, my point is that accountants define profit very differently than entrepreneurs do. They consider it as a yearly event, an abstract number at the bottom of another report. Put simply, they are only interested in your profit to calculate income tax.

Entrepreneurs define profit as surplus cash. Cold. Hard. Cash. Cash to invest. Cash to fund growth. Cash to pay dividends.

You can't pay bills with profit. Cash is the only thing that matters. So, the million dollar question is: Where is your cash?

I will help you find your cash. I'll will even show the best tactics that I know on how to maximize it.

To start, you need to know why your profit does not equal cash.

Accounting Profit is Misleading

If you're part of the 98% of the businesses that turnover less than $10M of annual revenue, chances are your 'accounting profit' is misleading. Why? Two reasons.

Your savvy CPA, Bob, has probably given you advice to deduct some personal expenses in your business, like the family car and, perhaps, home office rent. He may have also recommended some 'tax adjustments' to your accounts so that your CEO compensation is based on tax brackets, rather than market salaries. While these are not necessarily real 'business expenses' that your company has incurred, they are reflected in your Profit & Loss for tax purposes.

Furthermore, it's likely Bob has made some funky adjustments to your year-end accounts, further manipulating this profit. These adjustments are known as GAAP (Generally Accepted Accounting Principles). GAAP is a rulebook that governs accounting. It's an intimidating 4,000-page document with a set of accounting rules. If you've ever suffered from insomnia, reading the GAAP bible will certainly cure it.

The Flaws of GAAP

For a long-time there was no uniform method to present financials. Companies were free to present their numbers in whichever format they pleased. No balance sheet? No problem! But I'm sure you can imagine where this lack of standardization leads to.

As bonuses are often tied to financial performance, executives would often manipulate the financial statements and present them in the most 'ideal light'. The most common approach was to inflate profit and assets by some dodgy accounting.

As a result of these 'creative accounting' practices, trusting investors were often duped. I'm sure you're familiar with Enron—the most scandalous example of fake accounting. Their profits and share price skyrocketed at the same time they were going bankrupt. How does that make any sense? You'll find out soon.

The ability to manipulate accounting had catastrophic impacts to the global economy. The Great Depression in 1929, for example, was attributed to dodgy accounting.

With mom and dad investors losing bucket loads of their money due to fake accounting practices, the government implemented GAAP to right it. GAAP introduced consistency across financial reporting, in an effort to help investors understand 'what is real'. The intent behind this, at the time, was a good one.

The problem with GAAP, however, is that it hasn't quite solved the problem. GAAP is widely open to interpretation by accountants —often creating inconsistencies amongst financial statements.

The irony is that GAAP accounting is taking us further away from the truth. To keep up with emerging business models and financial loopholes, new accounting standards are invented every day. This makes financial statements even more complex for laymen (and us accountants) to understand.

The result is that the accounting profit on your financial statements isn't actually real. It's simply 'profit' according to GAAP. Bob the CPA spends his hours manipulating your profit to align it with GAAP. Not to benefit the success of your business.

So if your profit isn't real, what is?

It's important to know that Bob can only fiddle with your accounting profit, not your cash position.

You can fake profit, but you can't fake cash. Cash is the only thing we know is real.

Cash or Accruals Basis?

When you first started up your business, chances are your accounting system was a shoebox. Piles of receipts would accumulate in the top drawer until it came time to file your taxes. Your poor bookkeeper Sandra would frantically enter these documents into a spreadsheet or accounting system, which she would give to Bob to file your taxes.

If you are still doing this, it's likely you are on a cash basis of accounting. That means you record revenue and expenses when they are received or paid in cash. Say, for example, when you pay an expense—that's when you record it in your accounting system. When you've received money from your customers, that is when you record it as income.

Accrual basis, on the other hand, is when you record your revenue and expenses when you issue invoices or receive bills from those customers and suppliers. If you receive a telephone bill in the mail, and have not paid it, entering that expense into your accounting system represents an accrual-based system.

The main difference between accrual basis and cash basis accounting lies when revenue and expenses are recognized.

If you're a startup business and your annual sales are less than $250,000, cash basis accounting is okay. Once you grow beyond $250,000 of revenue you should move to accruals basis accounting. This is because as your business has more moving parts, you need a more accurate reflection of your financial performance.

Bank Balance Accounting

If you're like most entrepreneurs, I'm going to guess that the only accounting you do is what business author Mike Michalowicz refers to as 'bank balance accounting'. It goes something like this.

You check your bank balance once a day and see a bunch of cash. Yes! You're cashed up! You proceed to pay the stack of bills piled in your top drawer. The bank account starts to empty quickly, and your feeling of intoxicating wealth turns to one of gut-wrenching sickness. You realize you didn't leave enough money for payroll next week. You panic. You make calls to your debtors, you apply for another credit card. You do everything you can to scrape together a few extra thousand dollars to pay your staff—even if it means that you will forego your paycheck this month. We've all been there (myself included). It's not a pleasant experience.

I'm going out on a limb and guessing that you only look at your Profit & Loss occasionally. Maybe once a month? You've probably looked at a balance sheet before, based on your accountant's nudging, but couldn't figure out what the hell it's supposed to mean. You've heard of a cash flow report. You might have even tried to generate one from your QuickBooks. But, alas, you struggle to decipher what it's trying to say. Meaningless mumbo jumbo.

But I guarantee that you look at your bank account every day, right? It's the only thing that actually matters. Cash is king!

The amount of cash you have in your account might even dictate your decisions. If you have money, you can afford to hire that next staff member, or invest in that new piece of machinery. And, if you don't have enough money? Well, you have to fire the staff you just hired, or sell off that piece of equipment.

That's no way to run your affairs. At least, not for long.

It's okay; you're not alone. Bank balance accounting is the most common way that all business owners manage their finances.

The problem with this seat-of-the-pants technique, however, is that monitoring the ebbs and flows of your bank balance doesn't help you understand if you have a cash flow-producing business. It doesn't help you understand if you're profitable. And, lastly, it leaves no clues on how to improve your performance.

Cash is Hiding in Your Bedsheets

Did I get your attention? Good.

Actually, it's hiding in your balance sheet. Not your bedsheets. Though, your granny might claim that it's safer than the bank.

So, to answer your question as to why your profit never equates to the cash in your bank account. Well, I've found it for you. Your cash flow is hiding in your balance sheet.

Yep, I know what your thinking: the dreaded balance sheet. That confusing report you rarely look at, let alone tried to decipher. Just one big number on top, the same big number on the bottom.

I want to change your mind about the balance sheet.

While it's the least understood report by entrepreneurs, it's also the most important.

"It sounds extraordinary, but it's a fact that balance sheets can make fascinating reading."

Mary Archer

A BALANCE SHEET ISN'T JUST BS

See What I Did There?

A Profit & Loss shows how much profit (or how many losses) your business has generated over a period of time.

But a Balance Sheet is different because it shows your company's financial position at a single point in time. It's generally reported at a month-end date like December 31st, for example.

So what does it show? Your balance sheet summarizes the things that your company owns and owes—things like how much cash you have in the bank, who owes you money, how much you owe to suppliers, and the accumulated profit you have generated over time.

Accountants love reading balance sheets because they represent a scorecard of the financial health of your business.

I want you to think of it in the same way. A balance sheet tracks the significant numbers that occur in your business. In this case, the main sections are assets, liabilites, and equity.

You Want More Assets

Assets are good. You want to have lots of assets, as it is an indicator that you have a strong, healthy business.

More technically, assets are the things that you own and the stuff you are owed. Assets are anything that will generate future value to your company—whether that be increasing cash flow, generating new revenue streams, or becoming more efficient.

Types of assets include:

- Cash: your cash in the bank
- Accounts receivable: the money owed to you by customers
- Inventory: the stock you own
- Plant, equipment, and motor vehicles: the stuff you own
- Intangible assets: the costs of trademarks/IP and licenses
- Investments: the cost of any investments in another company

On a balance sheet, assets are split by Current and Non-Current.

CURRENT ASSETS

Current Assets are everything that you could possibly convert into cash within one year. We categorize assets like this because it helps to know what can be liquidated quickly to fund the day-to-day running of your business.

Current Assets include:

- Cash and deposits
- Accounts receivable
- Inventory

NON-CURRENT ASSETS

On the other hand, Non-Current Assets are physical items and intangibles that are more difficult to convert into cash quickly. They are comprised mainly of long-term assets and investments that your business leverages to produce future revenue.

Non-Current Assets include:

- Plant, equipment, and motor vehicles
- Trademarks and patents (intangible assets)
- Investments

It's Your Round

To demonstrate, I'll use a frame we're all familiar with. It's Friday night and you're at a bar having a few drinks with friends. It's your buddy Michael's turn to buy a round. He looks at you sheepishly and says he 'forgot' his wallet (we all have a friend like Michael). To help him save face in front of everyone, you lend him $100.

Now, the $100 Michael owes you would be listed as an 'accounts receivable' on your personal balance sheet. Accounts receivables are classified as current assets because you can get that money paid back relatively quickly... That's assuming Michael is good for it.

Now, compare this to owning your own house. Your house is classed as a 'non-current' asset on your personal balance sheet. It's non-current because if you want to sell it for cash, you can't dump it quickly. You need to get a real estate agent, find a buyer, go through legals and pest inspection, and then a settlement period.

It takes time to sell non-current assets. That's why they're called *non*-current.

Some Major Flaws with Your Assets

As we covered in the previous chapter, accounting has its flaws. Some of the biggest flaws are in your balance sheet.

IS IT AN EXPENSE OR AN ASSET?

When a company buys capital equipment, say a new car for the business, that purchase doesn't get expensed on the Profit & Loss. Instead, this new asset is accounted for on the Balance Sheet under Non-Current Assets. Accountants call this type of outlay Capex (short for Capital Expenditure).

Over time, the value of your car will be worth less. It gets some wear and tear; it loses its new car smell. Maybe the tires need replacing. This decline in value is in your P&L as 'depreciation'. Your CPA Bob will record this depreciation as a 'non-cash' expense on your Profit & Loss every year.

You might think there is a clear distinction of when you should directly expense equipment to the Profit & Loss, versus 'capitalize it' or record it as an asset to the Balance Sheet. GAAP has a whole section on what types of things should be allocated to each one. However, it's still very much open to interpretation. This leaves a lot of room for the manipulation of financial statements.

From an accounting perspective, allocating an expense to the balance sheet reduces your expenses, resulting in a higher profit. It also increases your asset position (remember, assets are good and we want more of them). The result is a double win.

This trick is adopted by dodgy companies that try to artificially 'improve' their financial results. Higher profits and more assets? The company must be crushing it, right?

WorldCom was one of those companies. The executive team did some 'creative accounting' by capitalizing all of the expenses related to the repairs of their assets. The result was fake accounting profit: $4 billion dollars of it!

Misinformed investors thought the company was doing well financially, and continued to invest in it—which inflated the share price further. Eventually, the bubble popped when WorldCom filed for bankruptcy in 2002, resulting in one of the largest corporate collapses in history. This happened barely six months after Enron, and it quickly transpired that both firms had been using the accounting services of Arthur Andersen. Despite being one of the 'Big Five' global accounting firms, Arthur Andersen was forced to surrender their CPA license and effectively close their doors as well.

So, what's the lesson here? Be aware of how your accountant and bookkeeper is accounting for your capital assets and large expenses. It can make a big impact to your profit.

"MARKET VALUE" IS VERY DIFFERENT FROM WHAT YOU PAID

It's important to also note that the value of the assets in your balance sheet is not often reflective of the price you can sell them for on the market—or 'market value'.

Instead, the value represents the price you paid to buy that asset on the date it was purchased: the cost price. This is really important as there are assets within your business that are valuable in the real world, which may not be reflected on the balance sheet.

Common examples include your brand or the value of intellectual property like trademarks and patents. This is a big flaw with traditional accounting, and an issue particularly relevant for tech firms. Technology businesses like Uber and Facebook have a high level of intangible assets like software, data, and brand value.

For accounting purposes, this value isn't reflected on the balance sheet, although they are highly valuable on the market. It's one of the reasons why tech company valuations don't make sense when trying to apply traditional financial measures.

Bottom line is that accounting is not perfect and is sometimes not a reflection of reality. It's important to be mindful of these flaws so you are better equipped to understanding what is real.

Liabilities

A liability is anything your company owes. They include funds you have borrowed from a financier, money owed to your suppliers, and your taxes that are due to be paid.

It's important to know your liabilities because you need to understand how much you owe to others.

Liabilities generally are comprised of:

- Accounts payable: money owed to suppliers and vendors
- Tax payable: amounts owed for taxes
- Loans: amounts owed to financiers

Like assets, liabilities are classed as Current and Non-Current, based on whether they are due to be paid within one year.

Current liabilities are debts payable within one year. These are the form of liabilities used to fund the day-to-day operations your business. They include:

- Accounts payable
- Credit cards
- Income taxes

Non-Current Liabilities are those that are due to be paid later than one year. They include:

- Mortgages
- Equipment loans

Equity

Equity is the value that your company owns. It's also referred to as Net Assets, because the value of your equity is your total assets less your total liabilities. It's the golden rule of accounting.

Equity includes:

- Retained profits
- Shares that are issued

We're not going to spend a lot of time talking about equity. If you focus on understanding your profit and loss, and your assets and liabilities, then the equity will take care of itself.

In summary, the balance sheet is a statement of what your company is owed, and what is owes. It's a scorecard of your firm's financial health at a certain moment in time. In the following chapters, I'll show you how to use it.

Your Cash is in the Balance Sheet

Remember how your current assets and liabilities are split by their ability to be liquidated into cash flow? These are important because they are the assets and liabilities used to fund the daily operations of your business. Accountants call this 'working capital'. That's because you need to put that capital to work!

Paying strict attention and managing working capital is key to ensuring that you are running an efficient, cash flow machine. For example, a company may have lots of assets and profit, but if it doesn't efficiently convert those assets into cash, you can end up with big cash flow problems.

Two Golden Rules of Working Capital Management

The key to unlocking your cash flow is to optimize your working capital. Your cash is tied up in the stock you have bought, the money that is owed by your customers. You also may have borrowed cash from your bank, and have credit card providers.

Working capital is stated as:

WORKING CAPITAL = CURRENT ASSETS – CURRENT LIABILITIES

To realize more cash flow in your business, remember these Golden Rules:

1. Decrease current assets
2. Increase current liabilities

Let's explore how we can practically do that in the next chapter.

"*What you search [for] is not necessarily the same as what you find. When you let go of the searching, you start finding.*"

Hermann Hesse

UNLOCK YOUR CASH

Growing Broke

"We just landed a half dozen new consulting clients, all five-figure engagements," Brendan tells me. "We're onto a record year of sales. But, my team are already doing crazy hours. I can't keep up with workload, and I simply don't have the cash to hire more staff. What am I doing wrong!?"

Growth is good. We all want and need to grow—to grow sales, to grow market share. But the problem with growing revenue is that costs grow with it. You need to hire more staff and buy more inventory. You might even want to rent more floor space. All of these expenses need to be funded… with cash.

Brendan at Voltage Media has been rapidly growing sales. This is great, right? The problem is that he doesn't have the cash flow to hire more staff to service his new clients. If Brendan continues to grow without fixing his underlying cash flow problem, he might not be able to pay his staff and other liabilities. If he can't pay his staff? Well, they'll probably quit and his business will implode.

Brendan runs the risk of 'growing broke'.

Technology startups grow broke all the time. They grow their sales and marketing teams, they grow their product teams. They grow their office space to include ping pong tables and beanbags. They burn through cash like the fuse on a stick of dynamite.

And if they fail to raise another funding round from their VCs?

Pop! It all implodes, and everyone moves onto the next disaster.

Here's the truth: the primary reason why startups fail is because they invest everything into growth, and risk running out of money. They grow broke.

This chapter is about how you can avoid that.

The 2 Golden Rules of Working Capital (Again)

Yes, I know that heading was already used. But I want to say it again because it's important.

As we covered in the previous chapter, your cash flow is tied up in Working Capital, which are:

- Accounts Receivable (current assets)
- Inventory (current assets)
- Accounts Payable (current liabilities)

You need cash to fund your growth, and paying strict attention to managing your working capital is the key to ensuring you are growing your revenue, profit, and cash flow—all at the same time. Working capital management is vital for high growth businesses.

If you're experiencing a cash flow crunch, it's best to remember The 2 Golden Rules of unlocking your cash:

1. Decrease Current Assets
2. Increase Current Liabilities

So, what does that practically mean?

I've outlined below a set of tactics you can implement to improve your working capital, and therefore cash flow. These tactics are universally applicable to both high-touch and low-touch business models, so pick and choose what best suits your company.

Golden Rule Tactic #1: Reduce Accounts Receivable

The first thing we're going to look at is how to reduce or eliminate your accounts receivable.

The greatest gains in realizing cash flow is speeding up the time it takes to collect cash from your customers. From experience, most companies have too much cash locked up in accounts receivable.

So, what is 'too much' accounts receivable?

If you have customers that owe you beyond their trade terms, you are leaving money on the table. It means you are lending them cash that should be in your bank account—not theirs!

To understand if you have a problem, we can quantify how many days it takes for your clients to pay. Here's how to calculate it:

STEP 1 – GENERATE A CURRENT BALANCE SHEET

Generate a balance sheet at the current time period and pay attention to the accounts receivable balance. This is also sometimes called trade debtors.

STEP 2 – DIVIDE THIS BALANCE BY MONTHLY SALES

Divide this balance by sales for the month.

STEP 3 – MULTIPLE THIS SUM BY 30

Multiple the sum from Step 2 by 30 (for the days in the month) to get an average number of days.

ACCOUNTS RECEIVABLE DAYS =
ACCOUNTS RECEIVABLE / MONTHLY SALES X 30

The result is the average number of days it takes for your customers to pay you.

You can then calculate how much each accounts receivable 'day' is costing you in potential cash flow, by the following formula:

CASH FLOW DOLLARS PER RECEIVABLE DAY =
ACCOUNTS RECEIVABLE / ACCOUNTS RECEIVABLE DAYS

Let's look at Voltage Media for a second. Brendan's problem is that while his sales and profitability are growing, he's struggling with his cash flow position. The problem is all his cash is 'locked up' in accounts receivable—the money owed by his customers.

I want to take a moment to diagnose where the damage is.

If you like, try it on your own business first. Hint: take Brendan's balance sheet below and apply the mathematics we did on the previous page, noting that his monthly sales figures are $200K.

Balance Sheet
Voltage Media LLC
For the year ended 31 December 2017

Current Assets	
Cash at Bank	$50,000
Accounts Receivable	$400,000
Total Current Assets	$450,000

Okay, if that's too much to think about right now, I'll do it for you. First, we need to go and calculate Brendan's current accounts receivable days.

1. CALCULATE ACCOUNTS RECEIVABLE DAYS

Accounts receivable days = $400,000 of accounts receivable/ $200,000 of monthly sales

X 30 days in the month.

Accounts receivable days = 60 days

2. CALCULATE CASH FLOW DOLLARS RECEIVABLE DAYS

Cash flow dollars per receivable day = $400,000 / 60 days
Cash flow dollars per receivable day = $6,666

What this means is that Brendan's customers take, on average, 60 days to pay him.

In addition, for every 1 day that Brendan's customers owe him money, it costs him on average $6,666 per day of missed cash flow.

This is pretty bad, given Brendan's invoice trade terms are 15 days. In other words, Brendan's customers are paying him 45 days late. If he could get them to pay him within their trade terms of 15 days rather than 60, it would realize $299,970 of cash flow (that's 45 days X $6,666 of cash flow days).

What a difference! He would have no problems hiring more staff with that cash flow.

High accounts receivables is the number one cash flow killer of small and growing businesses. As founders, it's easy for us to focus all our effort on sales. But that's only one part of the equation. We need to put equal effort into converting those sales into cash. Remember, you can't pay bills with sales. Cash is what matters.

So how do we practically do that? We'll get to that in a moment. But first, I want you to diagnose if you have an accounts receivable problem.

TAKE ACTION – CALCULATE YOUR OWN

Enough with the examples. It's time to grab a pencil and calculate your accounts receivable days.

Please use the cocktail napkin on the next page for your work.

If your average accounts receivable days are beyond your trade terms, you're leaving cash on the table. You need to collect what's due to you ASAP.

Think of it like a game: don't let the accounts receivable days get past your trade terms. It they're getting close, do what it takes to reduce them.

You can generate a list of the customers that owe you money via the 'aged receivables' report from your accounting system. That report will identify which customers owe you money, and how many days they are overdue past their scheduled due date.

What are Normal Accounts Receivable Trade Terms?

I've seen trade terms vary—from cash up front to even 90 days. There is no 'rule' and it largely depends on your industry and business model.

Low-touch business models, like e-commerce and Software as a Service (SaaS) businesses for example, often have no accounts receivables. This is because their customers pay upfront for the product via credit card or direct debit. That's why they are attractive business models to investors.

If you're in a high-touch business like professional services or manufacturing, your average trade terms are sometimes dictated by the clients you service. For example, Fortune 500 companies and governments often have the power to dictate large contracts which can be up to 60 or even 90 days. It can be more challenging to negotiate lower trade terms with customers that have the weight and upper hand to call the shots. But don't take it for granted; everything is negotiable.

Besides that, there are no rules on what trade terms you dictate to the market. My recommendation is always, the lower the better. Aim for 7 to 14 days max. It's your business machine: you must design what works for you.

Tactics on Chasing Debts From Your Customers

I've tested dozens of tactics on chasing accounts receivable (using my clients as guinea pigs). Here is the most effective tactic to call in your debtors that doesn't involve steel pipes and 'hired help'.

STEP 1 – HAVE SOMEONE (WHO IS NOT YOU) SEND AN EMAIL

Arrange for your virtual assistant or an administrator (finance officer) to send an email to your customer's finance department. The email should go something like this:

Dear X,
Our invoice for $10,000, dated on the 15 December is well overdue. We were expecting this to be paid when it was due on [insert due date]. Can you please advise when this will be paid. Our invoice is attached to this email for your records.

It's important that the email is not sent from you. Sending admin emails yourself screams start-up. Also, creating a degree of separation from yourself to your customer removes all possibilities for 'extended terms' or price disputes. Have your virtual assistant, office manager, or receptionist send the email and engage in all correspondence.

STEP 2 – CHILL FOR TWO DAYS

Let the email sit for 48 hours. Have your team member call the customer to follow up on your email to ensure they received it and ask when the payment will be made. Always ask for a payment date.

STEP 3 – ESCALATE IT!

If your team member is not having any luck getting through, get them to contact the manager in charge with whom you are dealing. The email should go something like this:

Dear X,

I'm [insert your name]'s accounts receivable officer. I want to make you aware that your company owes us $10,000 which is now well overdue. I know this is not your area, but I would appreciate it if you could please follow up on this payment. I will call you tomorrow if I don't hear a response.

STEP 4 – NO RESPONSE? RAMP IT UP

If you still don't get a response, then ramp it up. It's time for you, or someone senior in your team, to do the dirty work.

Call your contact and follow a script something like this:

Hello X,

Firstly I hate to waste your time, and mine, but I have a problem. My accounts team has contacted you several times with no response. Our account is well overdue and I expected it to be paid on [insert due date].

In our engagement letter you agreed to the terms and we have completed our contract. We fulfilled our obligation, but you have not fulfilled yours. I will have to cease all work if you cannot give me an expected date on when this will be paid.

The idea is to make this a bit more, shall we say, forceful. Don't hesitate to be the bad cop. If you still don't get any cut-through with that, cease all work and make them come to you.

Chasing customers for money always sucks and is, more often than not, disheartening. Nobody likes asking for money. Don't let the fear takeover. You are in control.

Tips to Never Have an Accounts Receivable Problem

As the saying goes: an apple a day keeps the doctor away. In other words, prevention is always better than the cure. Here's a few apples to ensure you never have an accounts receivable problem.

TIP #1 – REQUEST CUSTOMER DEPOSITS

Make your clients pay upfront for your services. If they are a returning customer, you have a good chance of getting paid up front. Try it. If that's not feasible for your customer, request at least a 50% deposit upon acceptance. The added benefit to this is to ward off 'flaky customers' who might not be serious about what you have to offer.

TIP #2 – GET YOUR CUSTOMER'S BANK DETAILS

There are an array of software applications that will securely store your client's bank account details and sync to your accounting system. I've listed these in the 'tools and tactics' section at the end of this Principle. Within your engagement letter/services agreement, attach a bank authority form which gives you permission to direct debit your customer's account.

On the invoice due date, you can automatically collect their payment via the application's payment platform. Many of these platforms have automated dunning as well, so it will automate the chasing of these debtors for you.

What happens if their payments bounce? Most software tools have triggers to debit their bank account. There is nothing more satisfying than hitting the 'collect now' on your invoices. It puts you in control of your cash flow.

TIP #3 – REMIND YOUR CLIENTS OF THE INVOICE DUE DATE

Cloud accounting software can send automated reminder emails to your customers. You can customize the email text, and send them based on the invoice due date. My recommendation is to automate reminder emails to your clients 3 days before the invoice is due, so they are reminded of your trade terms.

If Your Big Customers Won't Budge on Trade Terms

If your customers are government, large Fortune 500 companies, or other businesses that pretend to be 'big', you may feel yourself at their mercy. Seek to negotiate on your trade terms. You will surprise yourself, at times, by simply asking.

If your customers won't budge on terms—and you need the cash flow for growth—consider selling your accounts receivables. There are commercial finance companies and banks that will lend you money, using your receivables as collateral for the loan.

The amount you borrow is usually a fraction of your receivables balance (varies between 50% to 80% depending on the quality of your customers).

You can also sell these accounts receivables to them. This is known as factoring. Under this arrangement, the factor takes responsibility for the collection of the debt and any bad debt losses. It's generally expensive and is subjective to several hurdles, however it can be an effective way to convert receivables into cash, while not exposing the company to additional financing.

Golden Rule Tactic #2: Manage Your Inventory

Tim Cook, CEO of Apple, was not the most 'logical' choice to be Steve Jobs' successor. Many said that Cook wouldn't be the leader, as he and Jobs were polar opposite in terms of their skill set and leadership style. Jobs was the product, marketing, and innovation guru. Cook, on the other-hand, was the master of operations.

When Cook first started at Apple in 1998, he was tasked with fixing the company's poorly performing supply chain management —from manufacturing and logistics all the way to distribution. He famously turned Apple's disastrous manufacturing processes into the 'gold standard' for electronics-manufacturing efficiency.

According to Cook, inventory is "fundamentally evil."

"You kind of want to manage it like you're in the dairy business," he remarked. "If it gets past its freshness date, you have a problem."

This discipline with their inventory management has ranked Apple as world class for operational efficiency. In addition, it's also one of the most 'cash rich' businesses in the world—carrying over $250B of surplus cash.

Inventory-based businesses can learn a lot from Cook. It starts with inventory management.

Inventory is the Devil!

If you're in a low-touch inventory-based business—like ecommerce, retail, or manufacturing—you know that inventory management can make or break your business.

Inventory management is a science. It takes data and an acute understanding of the market to get the balancing act of inventory purchases just right.

If you carry too much stock, your cash becomes tied up. These funds could otherwise be used to fund the rest of your business. This cash flow problem can be compounded if your product is perishable or depreciates quickly—as it loses value each day you hold on to it. In a worst case scenario, you could be left with no cash and no product.

On the flipside, if you carry too little stock, you might run out and have nothing to sell to your customers. This can cripple your future sales, as your revenue is hamstrung until you can be restocked.

In the meantime, your impatient customers (who demand instant gratification) will be looking for alternatives—most likely from your competitors.

A key metric to help you manage your inventory and cash flow is a little something called 'inventory days'.

Inventory Days

Similarly to how you calculated accounts receivable days, you can also quantify inventory days. This metric tells you, on average, how many days you're holding your inventory before you sell it to customers.

Here's how to calculate it:

STEP 1 – GENERATE A CURRENT BALANCE SHEET

Generate a balance sheet at the current time period and take note of your inventory value.

STEP 2 – DIVIDE BY MONTHLY 'COST OF GOODS SOLD'

Divide this balance by the monthly 'cost of goods sold' value from your Profit & Loss for the month.

STEP 3 – MULTIPLY BY 30 FOR AN AVERAGE NUMBER OF DAYS

Multiply this by 30 (days in the month) to get an average number of days.

INVENTORY DAYS = INVENTORY VALUE / COST OF GOODS SOLD x 30

You can calculate how much cash can be unlocked for every day of inventory with the following formula:

CASH FLOW DOLLARS PER INVENTORY DAY =
INVENTORY VALUE / INVENTORY DAYS

Inventory days give you a quantifiable and data-driven approach to inventory management. It changes your mindset—from guessing how much inventory you have—to how long it will last until you have to make your next inventory order. It helps to manage your buying cycle times.

Let's take a look at Sarah's startup, Moo Formula, and review how we can improve her inventory days.

Balance Sheet
Moo Formula Inc.
For the year ended 31 December 2017

Current Assets	
Cash at Bank	$537,639
Accounts Receivable	$57,750
Inventory	$600,000
Total Current Assets	$1,137,639

Also, you should note that Moo Formula's purchases were $269,500 for the month of December 2017.

STEP 1 – CALCULATE INVENTORY DAYS

Inventory days = $600,000 of inventory /
$269,500 monthly purchases x 30 days in the month
Inventory days = 67 days

Now that we have a handle on the inventory days, let's calculate how much one inventory day costs in lost cash flow.

STEP 2 – CALCULATE CASH FLOW DOLLARS PER INVENTORY DAY

Cash flow dollar per inventory day = $600,000 of inventory /
67 inventory days
Cash flow dollar per inventory day = $8,955

That means that for every 1 day that Sarah holds in stock, it costs the company on average $8,955 per day of foregone cash flow.

Sarah should therefore aim to reduce the amount of inventory she holds to realize this cash flow.

TAKE ACTION – CALCULATE YOUR INVENTORY DAYS

Okay, now try it for yourself below.

What are Normal Inventory Day Benchmarks?

Average inventory days vary between industries and depends on the product type and business model. For example, companies that sell perishable or fast-moving products, like food, will have a lower inventory days benchmark than businesses selling non-perishable or slower-moving products, like cars.

Below is a guideline of inventory benchmark days for key industries from the 2010 issue of *Supply Chain Digest.*

Industry	Average Inventory Days
Internet and Catalog Retail	30
Restaurants and Cafes	3 to 5
Apparel and Luxury Goods	60
Consumer Technology	30

Every business is unique, so these inventory days benchmarks should be used only as a guide. For example, in 2017, Apple's average inventory days was a mere 11.18—an enviable figure, given that the benchmark for consumer tech is 30 days.

If your inventory days are higher than the benchmarks, consider ways you can reduce them. Lower inventory days result in more cash. It's one more goal as you strive for operational excellence.

Tactics on Reducing Inventory Days

Obsolete and slow-moving stock are the culprits behind bloated inventory balances. These are the products that have become dated because a newer, shinier version has been launched in the market.

The old stuff is no longer 'sexy'. When was the last time people were buying iPhone 5s? Your old stock is costing you money—not just the opportunity cost of valuable cash, but also indirect costs like warehouse space.

There are a number of methods to identify obsolete stock. You probably already have a feel for what needs to be written-off. For a data-driven approach, generate a stock report from your inventory management system and filter the data to identify the last sale date. If the time period from your sale date to today's date is greater than your Inventory Days metric, assess whether it can be sold at a discount price, or at worst case, written off completely.

Most third-party logistics providers generate these reports, so if you don't have an inventory management system, simply request it and do the same analysis.

Yes, selling obsolete stock may have an impact on short-term profits. But they will be offset by the long-term benefit as your carrying costs are eliminated, and immediate cash flow is realized. Ignore sunk costs.

Golden Rule #2: Increase Current Liabilities

As we saw, there are a bunch of different ways to improve cash flow under the Golden Rule #1 (Decreasing Current Assets). Our next Rule, however, is slightly less flexible.

There's only one thing we can do here: Push out your accounts payable into the future.

Extending your accounts payable is a tactic that requires you to pay your suppliers at a later date. Doing this allows you to cover your expenses without having to seek external sources of financing. This can be effective, but be warned.

Your accounts payables are your supplier's accounts receivable. Stretching a friendship too far can damage the relationship with your suppliers. Suppliers should be held in the same regard as your employees and even your customers—as without them you wouldn't have a business. If you decide to pursue this strategy, be conscious of their needs and seek their permission first before making any drastic changes.

Similar to accounts receivable days, accounts payable days are calculated using the same methodology.

$$ACCOUNTS\ PAYABLE\ DAYS =$$
$$ACCOUNTS\ PAYABLE\ /\ DIRECT\ COSTS\ x\ 30$$

You can calculate how much each accounts payable 'day' is costing you in potential cash flow, by the following formula:

CASH FLOW DOLLARS PER PAYABLE DAY =
ACCOUNTS PAYABLE / ACCOUNTS PAYABLE DAYS

Balance Sheet
Moo Formula Inc.
For the year ended 31 December 2017

Current Liabilities

Accounts Payable	$180,000
Taxes	$60,000
Total Current Liabilities	$240,000

And, once again, you should note that Moo Formula's purchases were $269,500 for the month of December 2017.

1. CALCULATE ACCOUNTS PAYABLE DAYS

Accounts payable days = $180,000 / $269,500 X 30
Accounts payable days = 20 days

2. CALCULATE CASH FLOW DOLLARS / ACCTS. PAYABLE DAY

Cash flow dollar per accounts payable day = $180,000 / 20
Cash flow dollar per accounts payable day = $9,000.

That means that for every 1 day that Sarah extends her accounts payable, she can defer on average $9,000 per day of cash outflow.

TAKE ACTION – CALCULATE YOUR ACCOUNTS PAYABLE DAYS

For effective working capital management, ideally your accounts payable days will be consistent with the trade terms of your suppliers. A good rule of thumb is 30 to 45 days.

Here are some pointers for extending your payable days.

- **Don't be an asshole. Everyone hates late payers.**

  Asking for extended terms is kind of like robbing Peter to pay Paul. You don't want to screw over your suppliers, because without them you don't have a business. Only extend your credit terms if you have to.

- **Everything is negotiable. Be up front with your reasons.**

  If you feel that the payment terms from your supplier aren't industry standard (or are just plain ludicrous), then seek to re-negotiate—particularly with new suppliers. Don't be shy to discuss pricing and payment terms.

Go ahead and calculate your Accounts Payable Days now.

So, how did you do?

Now that we've gone through some of the tactics, let's dive into how you can constantly monitor your cash flow.

"If you're trying to create a company, it's like baking a cake. You have to have all the ingredients in the right proportion."

Elon Musk

MAXIMIZE YOUR
CASH FLOW ENGINE

Combustion Engines

I've long admired the ingenuity of the humble combustion engine. They work like this: a blend of air and fuel is ignited by a spark plug, causing combustion within a cylinder. The force of this pushes a piston, which rotates a shaft, which turns a wheel.

An efficient combustion requires a lot of moving parts to operate perfectly in sync. In fact, 80% of an engine's performance boils down to getting the air to fuel ratio exactly right. Engineers and scientists have optimized the perfect ratio to be 14.7:1—that is, 14.7 parts air to every 1 part fuel.

Getting this exactly right is critical. Because if there's too much air, the engine will not produce enough energy in the combustion, resulting in less power. If there's not enough air, the engine generates more power, but burns through fuel.

Your company's cash flow engine works in a similar way. The profit generated by your business is the fuel. The air is the time it takes to combust that fuel. To maximize the cash flow power generated by your business engine, you want to shorten the time it takes to convert your profit into cash. In effect, starving your engine of air so it produces explosive cash generating power.

We call this the Cash Conversion Cycle.

In your business, the Cycle measures the number of days it takes to convert your profit into cash. It's a simple metric to measure the overall liquidity of your business operations. In essence, the fewer days it takes to convert your profit into cash, the better.

We can think about the Cycle in mathematical terms, being:

CASH CONVERSION CYCLE = ACCOUNTS RECEIVABLE DAYS + INVENTORY DAYS − ACCOUNTS PAYABLE DAYS

The best part about measuring the Cash Conversion Cycle is that you've already done the hard part. Remember, in the last chapter, when we calculated the average number of days on your accounts receivable, inventory, and accounts payable? Basically, the Cash Conversion Cycle pulls it all together so we get a complete view of your cash cycle.

Timing Your Cash Conversion Cycle

Let's look at Moo Formula as an example.

Working Capital Summmary
Moo Formula Inc.
For the year ended 31 December 2017

		Days
ASSETS		
Current Assets		
Accounts Receivable	$57,750	30
Inventory	$600,000	72
Total Current Assets	$657,750	
LIABILITIES		
Current Liabilities		
Accounts Payable	$180,000	21
Total Current Liabilities	$180,000	
Cash Conversion Cycle		81

Check out the napkin diagram below. It shows a timeline of the total number of days that Moo Formula takes to buy their inventory from suppliers, store it in the warehouse, sell it to their customers, and then eventually get paid.

Forgive my drawing, but it looks something like this:

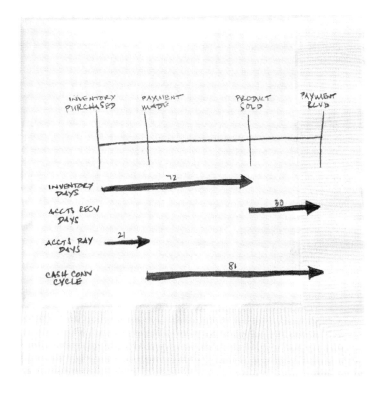

For 2017, Moo Formula's inventory days are 72 days, accounts receivable on wholesales products are 30 days and the company's accounts payable are paid in 21 days.

The net result is that it takes on average 81 days to convert all of the profit generated by the company into cash. This means Sarah's investors are financing 81 days of cash flow required for the daily running of the business.

Is that good or bad? To me, it's not great.

It's like the air valve in Moo Formula's cash flow engine has a kink. Sarah needs to focus on lowering her conversion cycle, so she can collect her cash faster and translate those sales into cash!

So, where should Sarah start? I'd suggest that she examine her inventory days (as they are the highest at 72), followed by accounts receivable days.

Again, you can lower these two accounts by implementing the tactics outlined in the previous chapter.

The Lower, the Better

The rule of thumb for a Cash Conversion Cycle is the lower the better. Lowering the amount of days it takes to convert your profit into cash means you can use the surplus cash to reinvest back into your business and avoid facing a cash flow crunch.

According to an analysis of Amazon's 2012 financial position by *Forbes*, the internet giant has a cash conversion cycle of -14 days. Yes, you read that correctly. It's negative!

Amazon manages to hold inventory for 28.9 days plus 10.6 days to collect receivables, then squares its accounts payable in 54 days. All together, this adds up to a cash conversion cycle of -14 days. That means that Amazon's suppliers are basically funding the operations of the business.

A negative Cash Conversion Cycle is a pretty rare thing, and raises some ethical questions about Amazon. A negative cash cycle is a win for Jeff Bezos and Amazon shareholders, but not for the myriad of suppliers waiting for their checks.

A Balancing Act

Fortune 500 companies are known to have terrible payment terms for their suppliers because they're trying to optimize their own Cash Conversion Cycle. But, remember, your accounts payable are your suppliers' accounts receivable.

It's a zero sum game, and there can be only one winner. You want to lower your Cash Conversion Cycle as much as possible, but you also don't want to screw over your suppliers for the sake of trying to squeeze out a few extra payable days.

Most of your cash will be tied up in Accounts Receivable and Inventory. Optimizing these two accounts will produce 80% of the gains in cranking your cash flow engine. Start with them.

"Accounting is the language of practical business life. But you have to know enough about it to understand its limitations, because—although accounting is the starting place—it's only a crude approximation. And it's not very hard to understand its limitations."

Charlie Munger

WARREN BUFFETT'S
SECRET SAUCE

It's Not Ketchup

Warren Buffett is regarded as the world's most successful investor. As chairman and CEO of investment conglomerate Berkshire Hathaway Inc., he runs the world's most valuable financial services company—posting revenues of over $200B in 2017.

In the investing world, Buffet is an outlier. Whereas hedge funds often undertake complex, high-frequency trading strategies, Buffett takes a radically opposite approach. Berkshire Hathaway's entire investment philosophy follows the Benjamin Graham school of value investing. That is, understanding the intrinsic value of a company, then buying it at a discount to their market valuation.

"Price is what you pay, value is what you get."

What's fascinating about Berkshire Hathaway's philosophy is that investment decisions are made using information, primarily in the form of financial reports and announcements, that is accessible on the internet and available to all of us. So, if Buffett has access to the same information we do, how does he continue to make sound investments and 'beat the market' in financial returns? What's the secret sauce to Buffett's success?

Critics and admirers say there are multiple factors that give him an edge. Firstly, Buffett is the master of controlling emotions. He doesn't get caught up in fads or short-term market fluctuations. He thinks long term and spends a lot of his time making decisions with careful consideration.

The second and most interesting factor is that Buffett interprets a company's set of financial statements differently to how you or I do. Through his unique analytical lens, he's able to spot patterns and trends that us laymen often miss.

Understanding how Warren Buffett views a company's financial performance leaves clues on how you can build a more valuable and cash rich business.

And, yep, it starts with numbers.

Cash Flow is the Source of Truth

Remember how accounting profit is misleading? Bob the CPA's idea of profit is prepared according to tax adjustments and GAAP. We learned that the guidelines of GAAP are very much open to interpretation for 'creative accounting'.

Dodgy CEOs and CFOs know all the tricks of the accounting trade. They know that the market can easily be duped.

The collapse of Enron is a prime example of how the assessment that investors make of a company's financial performance is guided by all the wrong numbers. In this case, the illusion of 'profit' while the company was actually entering bankruptcy fooled thousands of investors into thinking it was a valuable company.

The tale of Enron is the non-fiction version of Hans Christian Anderson's *The Emperor's New Clothes*.

The familiar fairytale is about a narcissistic emperor whose only concern in life was showing off how well-dressed he was. He cared nothing about his empire, but solely about looking good and letting the world know how 'great' he was. Vanity metrics.

He hired two weavers (actually con men) who convinced him to buy a new royal garment. They said it was made from a special, fine fabric that was invisible to anyone who either was unfit for their position or 'hopelessly stupid'.

Thus, when the emperor was sporting his new garment, nobody —including the emperor's trusted advisors and ministers—could actually *see* his alleged 'clothes'. But they dutifully pretended that they could for fear of appearing 'stupid' or unfit for their positions. The emperor, caught up in his own ego, did the same.

Now the day came when the emperor was to present his new garment in public—strutting butt naked down the middle of the street. All of his loyal subjects continued the charade for him, afraid to state the obvious. Everyone was caught up in the hype.

Then, a few blocks down the street, a child—too innocent to understand what the hell is going on—blurted out that the emperor was wearing nothing at all!

"Why is he naked?" the child wondered.

Like the emperor, Enron 'dressed up' their business with dodgy financial engineering, convincing the public (and themselves) that they had an awesome, profit-pumping business.

So, how can we be the child that calls bullshit on the ruse?

For a bit of fun, let's look at a summary of Enron's financials leading up to its collapse in 2001—which I've summarized on the next page. From a 'net profit' perspective, Enron was crushing it. It was profitable year-on-year with 12% compounded growth.

But if you take a look at the Net Cash Flow position, you will see that Enron was losing truckloads. Over the 4-year period shown, it only had one year of positive cash flow. You would think *that* alone would ring alarm bells for investors. But it didn't. They were too focused on looking at profit.

You can fake profit, but you can't fake cash.

Warren Buffett isn't fooled by companies like Enron, as he knows all the tricks adopted by companies to manipulate financial statements, and the flaws in accounting in general.

Accordingly, he's able to cut through the hype and wizardry to understand the truth behind a company's financial performance.

Summarized Cash Flow Position
Enron

(Millions $)	1996	1997	1998	1999
Net Profit	$584	$105	$703	$893
Non-Cash Expenses	$474	$600	$827	$870
Movement in Balance Sheet	$142	($65)	($233)	($1,000)
Capital Expenditures	($855)	($1,413)	($1,905)	($2,363)
Net Cash Flow	$345	($773)	($608)	($1,600)

One of Buffett's secrets is this: rather than looking at a company's ability to generate 'profit'—which can be so easily manipulated—he looks at a company's ability to generate cash flow.

Buffett pays close attention to a metric called Free Cash Flow.

Free Cash Flow: the Warren Buffett Metric

Free Cash Flow is a Frankenstein metric that considers accounting profit and cash flow. It's measured and assessed by investment gurus like Buffett because it gives a clearer view of a company's ability to generate positive cash flow.

A positive Free Cash Flow means your company is actually generating surplus cash. Negative Free Cash Flow means you're burning cash (hence the term Burn Rate).

What I love about Free Cash Flow is that it not only gives you an accurate view of your cash flow position, it also provides clues on how to improve it. It can help you understand what changes you need to make in order to unlock more cash.

Calculating Free Cash Flow

Free Cash Flow can be calculated by taking your net profit and adjusting it by any non-cash expenses, movements in your working capital (accounts receivable, inventory, and accounts payable)—and then deducting your capital expenditure.

FREE CASH FLOW = NET PROFIT + NON-CASH EXPENSES
– CHANGE IN WORKING CAPITAL – CAPEX

Let's take a practical example of calculating Free Cash Flow using Moo Formula.

Free Cash Flow
Moo Formula Inc.
For the 3 months up to 31 December 2017

	31-Dec-2017	30-Nov-2017	31-Oct-2017
Net Profit	($114,500)	($114,500)	($113,000)
Add: Non-Cash Expenses	$ -	$ -	$ -
Movement in Balance Sheet			
Accounts Receivable	$ -	$750	($3,000)
Inventory	($50,000)	$20,000	($26,667)
Accounts Payable	($70,000)	$50,000	$30,000
CAPEX	($30,000)	$ -	$ -
Free Cash Flow	**($264,500)**	**($43,750)**	**($112,667)**

A couple of things to note here:

- **Non-Cash Expenses** are depreciation, amortization, and bad debts. Your CPA, Bob, will typically account for these.

- **CAPEX** stands for Capital Expenditure. This is money spent on equipment like motor vehicles, plant, and equipment.

As you can see in the calculation (above), Moo Formula has negative Free Cash Flow—it's burning money.

In the month of December, the accounting loss was $114,500, however the Burn Rate for the period was $264,500. This is because there were a lot of payments made for inventory, accounts payable, and capital expenditures in that period.

Also, notice how there's a direct correlation to your Free Cash Flow and the movement in working capital? Effective working capital management means better cash flow.

Free Cash Flow Leaves Clues

I recommend that every business measure and monitor Free Cash Flow—even if your company is profitable. The primary benefit of assessing your Free Cash Flow is that it provides clues for how to improve cash flow.

For example, as Free Cash Flow considers the ebbs and flows of working capital (the accounts where your cash is hiding), drilling into these components helps you understand how to unlock this cash. If you're not confident calculating this yourself, ask your CPA or bookkeeper to help you generate a report from your accounting software.

Free Cash Flow is Uncommon to Measure

I know we beat up on Bob the CPA too much, but it's highly unlikely that Free Cash flow is reported in the financial statements prepared by him. Why? Because it's not legally required for small businesses.

Remember, financial statements are prepared in accordance with GAAP standards to ensure consistency. In other words, traditional financial statements are not designed to help entrepreneurs like you understand your finances.

This is why you need to see them stark naked, and calculate them for yourself!

"Cash is oxygen."

Gary Vaynerchuck

DON'T BURN YOUR RUNWAY

All You Can Eat

I'm a sucker for buffet restaurants. When food is plentiful and in abundance, I take 'all you can eat' a bit too literally.

I'm sure you're familiar with the routine: you stack your gigantic plate with the sheer variety of food and shove it down like it's your last meal. You repeatedly tell yourself that you should stop eating, but you can't help yourself. You continue to pick at it, until your belly is full to the point that it hurts to breathe.

You regret your decision to eat that last cupcake as you slowly recover from a self-induced food coma. That feeling of sickness from overeating and heartburn? It's not pleasurable. So why do it?

Turns out it's a cognitive weakness. Our brains are bound by our genetic legacy to our hunter-gatherer ancestors, who—uncertain of when they'd see their next meal—instinctively ate as much as possible, and whenever possible. The more food that's readily available to us, the more we eat. It's hardwired in our DNA.

The same concept goes for eating off big plates. We have the need to fill them excessively, and we don't register that the amount we're eating is actually more than normal.

It turns out this behavioral flaw actually applies to other areas in our life, including our finances.

Have you been in a position where you see a bunch of cash that has magically appeared in your bank account? Perhaps it was the payment of a large customer account, or even your first round of investment from a VC?

What's your reaction?

Wow! You're cashed up!

You feel good; you feel wealthy; you feel generous. You feel like spending it, quickly.

As humans, we have a natural tendency to spend money as we see it. This can get us into a lot of trouble financially when we burn cash on unnecessary things—even spending money that doesn't belong to us!

Cash Flow Dieting

To counter this, we're told by accountants and financial advisors that we should all maintain a 'financial budget'. Remember that?

There are few words in the English language that conjure up feelings of scarcity and deprivation more than the word 'budget'. Our lizard brain responds to the term in the same way it does to the word 'diet'—utter dread.

Budgeting, like dieting, sucks because it requires determination. It requires us to be disciplined with our spending habits. It forces us to think twice about spending and adopt the mentality of penny pinching. It often requires a big change in habits.

The tactic I'm about to share has nothing to do with that.

It's About Eating Off of Smaller Plates

After years of research, and over 50 studies, science says that the key to eating less food is to simply use smaller plates. In fact, studies suggest that halving plates size leads to, on average, a 30% reduction in the amount of food consumed.

Why? It's thanks to a powerful optical effect known as the Delboeuf Illusion. The illusion works because we think things are smaller when we compare them to things that are larger.

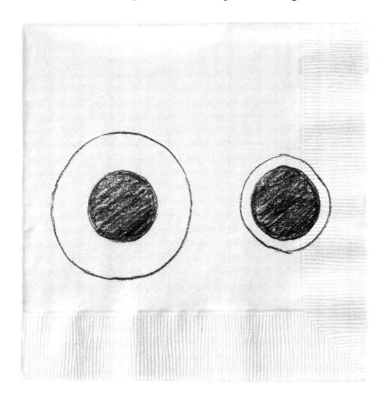

If you put a small amount of food on a large plate, your mind will tell you that you're eating an inadequate portion. Your lizard brain automatically drives you to add more food to 'fill' the plate. However, if you put that same amount of food on a small plate, your mind will tell you that you are eating a large portion and you'll stop adding additional food.

We can also apply this psychological hack to your finances by keeping your cash split among multiple bank accounts. Dividing your cash is the equivalent of eating off smaller plates of food.

Here's my recommendation on how you should manage it, so you don't let your buffet brain get out of control.

STEP 1: SETUP SEPARATE BANK ACCOUNTS

I suggest that you have, at minimum, 3 business bank accounts. Set them up as follows:

1. Operating account: for transactions
2. Taxes: a savings account
3. Profit/Investment account: more savings

The Operating account is for your day-to-day transactions: receipt of income, payment of bills, salaries, and the like.

The Tax account is used for payment of taxes. Remember, all the cash you receive from your customers doesn't belong to you. Some of it belongs to Uncle Sam, in the form of employment taxes for your staff and, quite often, sales tax as well.

The Profit/Investment account is used for holding any surplus cash, like any investor funds and cash profit.

STEP 2: TRANSFER TAXES & SURPLUS CASH TO ITS OWN ACCOUNT

At the end of each month, generate a taxes report from your accounting system to understand the employment taxes accrued for the period and transfer this value to the tax bank account—and don't touch it! Budgeting for this now will save you a ton of stress come tax filing time.

Ensure that all surplus cash flow is held in the Profit/Investment account. Transfer money to and from this account as you need it. The idea of this account is to hold surplus funds so you don't spend it, as you do your general operating expenses.

By splitting your cash among multiple bank accounts, you are in effect creating a budget for the cash used in your business. It creates a psychological barrier to burning through your cash à la buffet restaurant style. Instead, you can eat like a Jenny Craig dieter.

Remember, if you can't resist temptation to spend your sweet cash—remove it completely.

How Do You Calculate Burn Rate?

If you are running a negative cash flow business, you are burning money. Your Burn Rate is an important and frequently asked question by investors in startup land, because essentially you are losing your investor's money.

The most common question I'm asked by startup founders is how to accurately calculate the monthly burn rate. Unfortunately, there is a lot of poor advice in the market about how to calculate it. It should seem obvious, right? I mean, isn't it just how much money you're losing each month? That's a misconception.

Listen closely. Your Burn Rate is the same calculation as Free Cash Flow. If you have negative Free Cash Flow, it means you are burning cash. Looking solely at accounting losses according to GAAP is not an accurate reflection of your Burn Rate, because it doesn't consider working capital adjustments and any expenses capitalized on your balance sheet. Remember, profit and cash are not the same thing.

So, if you're burning cash flow, the next obvious question is how long do you have before you run out of cash?

Startups and Burn Rates

Before we continue, I want to clear something up. The following recommendation is applicable to 'startups'—business models which are typically low-touch. In popular culture, a startup is scalable, higher risk, and almost always technology-based. Think of brands like Uber, Facebook, and Snapchat.

Quite often, startups can't get access to funding from traditional banks or lenders due to their risk profile. Accordingly, they generally get access to money from investors—be that friends and family, angel investors, or venture capitalists.

If you run a business that is not a startup, like a digital agency or a restaurant, focusing on the profit levers and cash flow tactics should help you with your cash flow issues. Don't consider raising any capital from investors to spend on growth until you have fixed these issues. If your business is a leaky bucket, adding more cash will not generate better financial returns.

Okay, let's continue.

The World's Most Dangerous Runway

Lukla Airport, in Nepal, is rated as the world's most dangerous airport. Nested in the base of the Himalayas, the airport is a mecca for ambitious hikers embarking on their expeditions to trek to the peak of Mount Everest.

Lukla is regarded as the most dangerous airport for two reasons. Firstly, the runway length is incredibly short at 1,729 feet. To give you an idea, runways at large passenger airports are at least 6,000 feet in length. The other reason why Lukla is dangerous is because it's built on the edge of a cliff. If a plane overshoots the runway, it risks flying straight into a mountain.

You couldn't fly a Boeing 747 into Lukla. The only aircraft suitable for this runway are those little twin-propeller planes. They seat around 20 passengers, and flying in one is akin to being crammed into a fridge with wings. How do I know this? Because I've been there. If you have aerophobia, I wouldn't recommend it for your exposure therapy sessions.

Airport runways are very much like a startup's runway. If you are flying a commercial 747, you will need the runway length to safely take off. If it's too short, you risk crashing and burning. If it's too long, it's wasted money on a redundant tarmac.

Instead of distance, startup funding is measured in time. Every startup that isn't profitable (i.e. all of them) has a certain amount of time left before their money runs out. This is referred to as your runway. A runway is a good metaphor because it's a reminder that when the money runs out, you're going to be dead or airborne.

The science of building your startup's runway is about raising just the right amount of cash needed to help you do just that.

Rockets Don't Need Runways, They Use Launchpads

It was 2008, a year Elon Musk describes as the worst of his life. Tesla was on the verge of bankruptcy. SpaceX had literally burned through all of its $100 million investment, with three of their previous rockets exploding before reaching orbit. Musk was in a severe financial crisis.

> "I could either pick SpaceX or Tesla or split the money I had left between them. That was a tough decision. If I split the money, maybe both of them would die. If I gave the money to just one company, the probability of it surviving was greater, but then it would mean the certain death for the other company."

At the eleventh hour, Musk managed to scrape some money together from himself and investors to keep Tesla alive. The deal ended up closing on Christmas Eve, just hours before Tesla had to make payroll.

As for SpaceX, his saving grace was winning a $1B contract with NASA to become a supplier to the International Space Station, announced just days before Christmas.

Crack the champagne! Musk managed to save both of his companies from imploding.

My question to Musk is why did he wait until so late to raise his round of funding for Tesla and SpaceX? If he started the capital raising process earlier in the year, would there have been a lot less stress for all parties involved?

I don't know the answer, but I could speculate that it was poor timing. Or that the CFO didn't watch the company's burn rate. Either case, the lesson here is you don't want to be like Elon. You need to know your runway, so you can plan for it.

Calculating Your Runway

To calculate your runway, take the current cash at the bank and divide it by your most current month's burn rate. If your burn rate fluctuates, take an average for the last three months. The point is is to get an approximation of how many months of cash you have left.

Runway Calculation
Moo Formula Inc.
at 31 December 2017

	31-Dec-2017	30-Nov-2017	31-Oct-2017
Free Cash Flow (or Burn Rate)	($264,500)	($43,750)	($112,667)
Average Monthly Burn Rate	($140,306)		
Current Cash at Bank	$537,639		
Runway (months)	3.8		

In the example above, Moo Formula has just under 4 months of runway left before the company runs out of cash. Should Sarah be concerned? Um... I would be.

When it comes to raising money, there's no 'rule book' of how much money you need to raise, but there are guidelines. For seed stage startups, having an 18-month runway is a good default. This allows for 12-15 months of time for your new venture to hit the performance targets you promised to investors. Then, you still have 3-6 months to start the capital raising process for Series A.

Capital raising can be a long, arduous process. Leave yourself a lot of time and room to fail. Don't be like Elon in this instance.

Help! I'm Running Out of Runway!

Startups burn cash. The classic way they do this is by hiring a lot of people fast—developers, sales teams, growth marketers.

More people = more payroll = higher burn rate.

When it comes to the interplay between your company's burn rate and hiring, Paul Graham, the co-founder of Y Combinator, has a few general suggestions:

(a) Don't hire people if you can avoid it
(b) Pay people with equity rather than salary
(c) Hire people who are going to write code, or
(d) Hire people who will go out and get users

In the high-tech startup world that Graham lives in, coders and users are the only things you need at first.

In Principle 4, I will offer financial tactics to help you understand when you should and can afford to hire more staff.

And what about firing them? We'll cover that, too.

Principle 3 Takeaways

- Profit does not equal cash. Accounting profit is sometimes a misleading metric measure, due to GAAP and tax adjustments made by your CPA. Keep these limitations in mind when you review your financial statements.

- Your Balance Sheet is not BS. It's a scorecard of your company's financial health. Pay particular attention to your current assets and liabilities as they help you understand your liquidity.

- Your cash flow is locked up in the balance sheet, especially in working capital. The Golden Rules are to decrease current assets and increase current liabilities.

- The Cash Conversion Cycle measures the average number of days it takes to convert your profit into cash. The rule of thumb is: the less days, the better.

- Accounting profit can be misleading. Free Cash Flow is a metric that reveals what's real. It helps you understand if your business is generating positive cash flow.

- Cash flow management is linked with behavioral psychology. Remove the temptation to spend cash freely when you have it. Remember to use smaller plates.

- Your burn rate is your Negative Free Cash Flow. Your runway is the amount of time before you run out of cash.

- Know how long your runway is, so you don't end up with cash flow headaches like Elon Musk.

SOFTWARE TOOLS FOR PRINCIPLE 3

Accounts Receivable automation tools:

- Chaser: http://chaser.io

- Debtor Daddy: https://debtordaddy.com

Accounts direct debit tools:

- UCollect: https://ucollect.biz/

- Invoice Sherpa: https://www.invoicesherpa.com

Accounts Receivable automation tools:

- Chargebee: https://www.chargebee.com

- Chargify: https://www.chargify.com

- Zuora: https://www.zuora.com

Principle 4

LEVERAGE YOUR ASSETS

EMPLOYEES ARE YOUR GREATEST ASSET

To create a valuable business, you must focus on building
and leveraging assets. I'm not just talking about physical assets
like your equipment. Hint: People are assets as well.

"Your company's most valuable asset is how it is known to its customers."

Brian Tracy

ASSETS ARE MORE THAN STUFF

Fancy a Coffin for a Bed?

If you're claustrophobic, don't stay at a capsule hotel.

A typical room is about 7 feet in length, and 3 feet in width and height—slightly larger than a coffin. It has a small compartment to store your shoes and purse, but not much else. The rest of your belongings are kept in external lockers next to the bathroom, shared with other residents.

Capsule hotels are not for everyone, but in Japan—where major cities are notoriously expensive—they're a low-cost alternative for travellers. And local businessmen too drunk to get home.

Capsule hotels were invented to accommodate 'salaryman'—a term for Japanese white-collar businessmen known for working hard and partying even harder. The hotels were designed as a Plan B option for those who'd rather stay for another round of beers, rather than catch the last train out of the city. Pretty cool, huh? A lot of people think so; they've become mainstream.

Capsule hotels are exploding across the Western world. This once-niche accommodation option is being installed in a number of airports. Have an awkward 8-hour layover?

No problem—rent a coffin to catch some shut-eye.

I marvel at the ingenuity of capsule hotels. Not only are they fun and a bit weird, they are a business model that prints cash.

Hotels are Hard

It's capital intensive to start a hotel business. For starters, you have to build the hotel. If you're fortunate enough to buy an existing one, it will probably be run down and require a big investment to fix.

Once you've got your operation up and running, you need an army of staff on rotation to cover the 24-hour room service, the onsite restaurant, housekeeping, and concierge. No matter how many guests stay on any given night, you still need to maintain your standards and deliver the same customer experience— whether that's for one person or one hundred.

A veteran hotelier knows that the key to running a successful hotel operation is all about occupancy rates. It's vital to ensure that occupancy rates are as high as possible so the rental income covers the fixed costs of running the hotel, plus some profit.

Hotel occupancy rates fluctuate somewhere between 50% to 80%. The fluctuation is primarily due to seasonality.

Capsule hotels buck this trend. This is because their occupancy rates are consistently above 80%, irrespective of the season. Because they're not for everyone. They cater to a small, focused niche market—overworked, drunk business people.

It's also less capital intensive to build a capsule hotel. As rooms are literally stacked on top of each other, they use a lot less land and cost less to build. Factoring the financial investment made into the building of capsule hotels, they generate above-average returns because they are a highly-leveraged business model.

Your Business is Like a Hotel

Frame your business in the same way. You may have some fixed assets like plant and equipment, machinery, vehicles. You will no doubt have some fixed costs, like your employees. These assets and costs are necessary investments in your business, because without them, you wouldn't have a product to sell.

Like a hotel operator, your focus as an owner is to utilize these assets to their full capability. To leverage them so they generate a financial return and create value to your organization.

The thing is your assets are not just stuff. They're not just the photocopier, machinery, and random equipment that Bob the CPA allocates on your balance sheet.

Assets are also your employees.

In Principle 2 we learned about how to drive profitability using your Three Profit Levers. Remember those? As a recap, they are the Sales Lever, Direct Costs Lever, and Operating Expense Lever.

When it comes to costs management, we learned that the lever we should aim to optimize is your Direct Costs Lever. Direct costs are typically variable in nature, meaning they increase and decrease in relative proportion to the volume of revenue that you generate in your business.

But what happens if we have already done what we can to reduce our direct costs? We're left with some tough questions about what to do with our Operating Costs Lever. The challenge with operating costs is that they are fixed costs. When I say fixed, I mean to say that irrespective of the sales volume being produced in your business, the costs will stay the same.

Employees are your Biggest Fixed Cost

Wages and labor costs are the often the largest fixed expense for a business. The challenge is that the state of your business doesn't matter, your staff still get their weekly pay check.

Like a hotel operator, the key to running a high-performing business is all about leveraging your fixed assets. This Principle is all about people. Because while people are technically fixed costs, they are your greatest asset, and you need to consider them in the same frame.

"*People are definitely a company's greatest asset. It doesn't make any difference whether the product is cars or cosmetics. A company is only as good as the people it keeps.*"

Mary Kay Ash

MAKE YOUR EMPLOYEES INDISPENSABLE

Employees are Your Greatest Asset

The most important asset at your company isn't something you can put your hands on. It isn't equipment or the physical plant, and it isn't data, technology, or intellectual property.

The most valuable part of your company is the people. Your employees are your greatest asset.

In fact, they're the best kind of asset. The more you invest in them, train them, nurture them, and lead them, the more valuable they become to you and your business. Unlike machines which depreciate over time, employees *appreciate* in value.

So why don't all CEOs consider them in this way? Why do you continually hear about companies that churn through staff like replaceable cogs in a machine?

I know part of the problem. It's because employees can be seen as dispensable expenses.

Although your employees are 'assets' in the real world, in 'accounting land' they are expenses on a Profit & Loss.

Your accountant sees them as names and numbers on a report— that can simply be eliminated.

Unfortunately, their value gets lost in translation.

How Do You Put a Financial Value on Linchpins?

Picture your most valuable team member. She leads, she connects others, she makes things happen. She creates order out of chaos. She is the one that figures out what to do when there's no rule book. She delights and challenges her customers and peers. She loves her work and pours her best self into it.

I'm talking about an employee who's a Linchpin. A what?

It's a term first coined by Seth Godin in his bestselling book *Linchpin: Are You indispensable?*

A Linchpin is a person who is literally indispensable to your organization. They're the type who doesn't go down a well-defined path, instead they make informed choices. They make a difference.

You know the key employee that you would do anything to keep and retain? That's a Linchpin. She adds so much value to your business that you could never put a price on her contributions.

I have a few Linchpins in my business. I bet you do, too.

It begs the question: How do you calculate a financial value for someone that is 'priceless'?

Well, the answer is you can't. Even if you tried, it would be too open to interpretation and manipulation. Dealing with GAAP is complicated enough; we don't need any more ambiguity.

So, to make things simple, your employees' wages are always expensed as 'payroll' in the Profit & Loss statement.

But this doesn't change our way of thinking.

High Leverage Activities

As the CEO, your most important role is to ensure you're getting the utmost from your staff, to lead them so they are empowered and will pour their best selves into their work.

We've all read the studies that a happy, engaged team will perform better and be more productive. It's common sense, really.

This is your leverage: having your staff produce more output with the inputs provided (such as time).

From an accounting perspective, we can quantify how leveraged your business is using a metric called Revenue per Employee.

Since wages are typically the highest fixed cost of every business, revenue per employee measures how effectively you are generating a return from your 'investment.'

You can calculate it yourself by taking your total sales and dividing it by the number of employees you have.

REVENUE PER EMPLOYEE = TOTAL REVENUE / # OF EMPLOYEES

The premise with revenue per employee is the higher ratio the better. In other words, a low revenue per employee metric indicates that your business is inefficient. This is because you are solving problems by throwing more people at it.

A high revenue per employee means you are leveraging people, systems, and brand equity to generate revenue. This is easier in some sectors than others. For example, tech giants like Google and Facebook boast revenue per employee values of over $1M.

How? They only hire the best and brightest, and those folks build scalable technology services. They have a high output team.

Revenue per employee isn't a leading indicator of success, but a lagging one. It's also a metric that's directly affected by significant waves of hiring, employee ramp time, maturity in a market, and many other factors. Accordingly, the revenue per employee metric will vary across industry and the phase of your business.

If you have a high-touch business model (and your goal is to build a profitable business), you should be targeting a revenue per employee metric of at least $200K to $230K revenue.

This implies you are leveraging your employees by a factor of 2x-3x, assuming that your staff's average compensation is in a range of $80-$100K annually.

On the other hand, low-touch business models are, by their very definition, less reliant on people and more scalable. For these types of companies, the sky is the limit.

Let's consider Brendan as an example.

Review the P&L for Voltage Media. As at year end on December 31st, the company had $2,400,000 of annual sales and 16 employees (including Brendan himself).

Profit & Loss
Voltage Media LLC
For the year ended 31 December 2017

Revenue	$2,400,000
Direct Costs	$1,350,000
Gross Profit	$1,050,000
Gross Profit Margin	44 %
Less Operating Expenses	$750,000
Net Profit	$300,000
Net Profit Margin	13 %

To calculate Brendan's revenue per employee, we simply divide the annual sales by the number of staff.

$2,400,000 / 16 employees
Revenue per employee = $150,000

The result is that each employee generates, on average, $150K of revenue. For the sake of simple math, let's assume that Brendan is paying each of his team members $100K annually. In this instance then, the company is generating a 1.5x leverage on each employee.

However, as a high-touch business, Brendan should be targeting at least $200K of revenue per employee to ensure he's at least getting 2x financial leverage on average per team member.

What are the reasons why Brendan is under-performing on this metric? He's either servicing clients inefficiently, he's not pricing his services properly, or he has too many employees. Maybe all three. Voltage Media needs to get more leverage from its staff.

What's your revenue per employee? Calculate yours now.

If you're above this metric—that is, in the sweet zone with a 2x-3x ratio—and your business is profitable, then great work! Give yourself a pay raise.

If you're falling below this metric, you need to consider tactics on how to increase your employee leverage. Luckily, take a peek at the name of the next section.

Getting More Leverage from Your Employees

In a high-touch business model, the value created for customers is a direct result of a person's output. This is common for consulting business models, such as accounting firms and digital agencies.

To understand each employee's utilization, we can analyze the amount of hours they spend creating value for clients versus the total time they spend working in the business.

For example, if one of your employees is at work for 8 hours a day and spends 4 hours creating value for a client; 2 hours in internal meetings; and 2 hours on lunch, coffees, and chatting with friends; then that person would be '50% utilized'.

At a very simple level, a 50% utilization rate means that only half of an employee's time at work is spent creating value for a client which results in any revenue being earned.

Of course the more productive an employee actually is, the more revenue that is generated.

On face value it may look like I'm being too, shall we say, unreasonable. Because, at a more complex level, perhaps those 2 hours spent in internal meetings were necessary for running the business. Side note: This is why I hate meetings.

Anyway, my point is a rational business owner wants their employees to be as productive as possible. Productivity = leverage.

How to Increase Employee Leverage

I'll cut right to the chase and say it: timesheets.

I know you're squirming in your lounge chair right now. I can feel the rage building up inside you.

It's okay, I don't blame you—because timesheets suck.

Take a deep breath and chill for a second. Get up and make yourself a cup of tea if you have to.

Go on, do it now.

Are you back? Let's continue.

You're probably thinking how your business will end up like a stale old accounting firm if you implement timesheets, and to some extent you're right. Timesheets can have a big impact on culture.

In my technical accounting days, I dreaded the timesheet. You take a personal phone call, grab a coffee, and go to the bathroom and there's half an hour you can't put to billable hours.

The pressure by management to hit my utilization target of 95% (or some other unrealistic number) week on week, inevitably lead to some creative entries when pondering what the last 15 minutes were spent doing.

I detested timesheets so much, I used to put random narrations in my 'non-billable' timesheet entries. It was a protest, in addition to natural curiosity to see if anyone actually read them. I even had cryptographic acronyms:

- UM: Useless Meeting
- AUMx2: Another Useless Meeting About Meetings
- LL: Liquid Lunch
- BS: Buying Snack
- ES: Eating Snack
- ITE: Inventing Timesheet Entries

Yeah, timesheets suck. But it doesn't have to be this way.

Necessary Evil

First allow me to explain why timesheets are important.

Timesheets are an important way to collect data about your business. For example: How many hours last year were spent doing proposals? How many doing client rework and revisions? How many lost hours due to IT issues? Perhaps you can't answer that. But, if you could, it would reveal some very interesting information.

Maybe the amount of rework you're doing means that you're under-quoting on jobs? Maybe that old hardware you've been putting off replacing is actually costing you more in lost time than to replace? Maybe there's one particular person who's taking a bit longer than usual to get something done and they could use some training or help?

The point of timesheets isn't to watch your employees' every move, it's to gather crucial data about your business. It's for this reason that you would be crazy not to use them.

Timesheets Suck. This is How to Do Them Properly.

I've thought about this. A lot. Part of me knows accounting and legal firms can be so profitable because they know where all their time is going—down to every 6 minute increment.

The other part of me remembers how much I hated having to keep track of every… single… minute.

Here's how to implement timesheets and still maintain a positive and creative culture.

TIP 1: TALK ABOUT IT FIRST

If you've never used them before, educate your employees about why timesheets are being implemented.

Recognize from the outset that this could be a significant cultural change for some of your people.

Shifting to timesheets is hard.

Like changing any behavior or habit, some people will resent it. Others will simply forget to fill the timesheets out.

If you explain to your team that you're more interested in the data around how the business is performing as opposed to if the staff are slacking off, then everybody will feel more comfortable.

TIP 2: USE 15-MINUTE TIME BLOCKS (OR LARGER)

Don't require time to be kept in blocks that are too specific, such as 6 or 10 minutes. It's not nice, it's not practical, and it's simply not necessary.

In fact, if my suggestion of 15-minute blocks already feels like too much effort, then base your timesheet entries around broader changes in activities.

When all is said and done, if a few minutes here and there go unaccounted for it's not the end of the world. Don't start breaking people's balls about it. Consider it a given that some amount of time will go 'missing' on normal day-to-day life activities (like tea and coffee, conversations, and bathroom breaks).

TIP 3: REVIEW TIMESHEET DATA AS A GROUP

Once a month get your employees together and review the data. Encourage them to explore ways to improve how things are getting done, to level up on your team processes.

For example, perhaps a lot of time is being sunk into something like proposals. If so, the people doing those proposals might have some great ideas on how to improve that. Perhaps the account managers are noticing that certain clients are more painful to deal with than others. Maybe the business would be better off not servicing those types of customers.

Without this data—and reviewing it as a collective—you will not get these valuable insights like this to aid in decision-making. Furthermore, engaging your employees in the process will help them see just how useful timesheets are to the team's success.

Nobody likes being micro-managed, especially if they are being watched by some variation of an Orwellian dictator.

Give your team enough emotional space to subscribe to the timesheet process. Everyone will be better for it.

Service-Based Businesses and Pricing Hourly Rates

A common question that I'm asked by owners of service-based businesses is how should they should price hourly rates. Do other firms just invent a number out of thin air?

Well, kind of. The best companies I know price the customer.

You should always charge on value, not by the time it takes to complete a project. Of course, this isn't always reasonable. Some clients want the 'old school' way of pricing a job based on time input. If you're in a situation that doesn't provide flexibility to price on value, here's a data-driven method to determine an hourly rate.

As a rule of thumb, your revenue-generating employees should be bringing in 2x to 3x their salary cost. At a fundamental level, this implies that your gross profit margin as a whole business should between 50% to 70%.

Using this multiplier, you can reverse engineer the charge-out rate based the number of hours worked each year and the expected number of billable hours.

Let's use Brendan's agency as an example.

Hourly Rate Calculation
Voltage Media LLC
For the year ended 31 December 2017

Employee - Salary Mulitplier 3.0 x	Employee annual salary	Target Revenue
Kirsten	$100,000	$300,000
# of Working Days per Calendar Year	260	
Hours per Working Day	8	
Total Available Working Hours	2,080	
Target Utilization Rate (85%)	1,768	
Charge-out Rate (at 85% Utilization)	$170	

What do the numbers tell us?

Well, based on an employee salary cost of $100K annually and a salary multiple of 3x, this employee should be targeting to generate $300K of annual sales for Voltage Media.

Assuming the employee works an 8-hour day and is utilized 85% of time, the firm's rate should be $170 per hour.

Remember that the hourly rate and utilization rate are leading indicators to the revenue per employee metric. Pay attention to these two levers if you have challenges with maximizing financial leverage on your employees.

WHEN CAN I AFFORD TO HIRE MY NEXT EMPLOYEE?

Hiring and Managing Staff

sigh...

Despite my ramblings about employees being your biggest asset, they're also the most challenging part of owning a business.

Why is it so hard?

You spend months finding the right person for the role. You convince them to leave their current job and join your mission. Once they come onboard, you spend thousands of dollars on training and coaching—hoping they will stay engaged, motivated, and inspired. Then, they leave. And you do it all over again.

It's not just the financial costs that make hiring difficult—it's the recruitment and onboarding costs, the new laptop, and company swag. All the stuff you do to set them up for success.

For me, what's hard is the mental burden that comes with employees. Knowing that I am responsible for their personal and career development, their finances—really, their entire livelihood.

When my staff tell me they're having babies and taking on mortgages, I try to smile and be grateful. I love progress and I feel blessed that I can help my team progress in their lives. But behind closed doors, I'm secretly freaking the f*&k out.

Because, now, the burden becomes greater. My staff need that monthly paycheck more than ever. And if I can't make my business work to deliver on the promise I've made to these people, I fail them. Even if those circumstances are outside of my control—like the economy tanking or a natural disaster destroying the office—ultimately, I am still responsible.

You're Fired!

Management and culture aside, what I've found to be equally as challenging is not just recognizing who to hire, but *when* to hire.

If you hire too early, you run the risk of having idle staff. They sit twiddling their thumbs with not enough meaningful work and projects to keep them engaged. If you hire too late, your current team members could burn out on the overload of assignments.

You risk poor quality work, missed deadlines, and unhappy customers.

It's a balancing act.

There are countless business books on finding the right people to join your team: books on management, culture, and leadership. They're all great and contain powerful frameworks for those things.

But the problem I've found is that there is limited advice for people to understand whether they *should* employ more staff. Or better yet, if they can afford to. It's the question of when.

Too many times have I seen businesses go through waves of hiring—getting excited about growth, only to let those people go twelve months later because the company didn't have the cash to make payroll.

I've been there. Chances are you have, too.

Donald Trump makes it look cool to fire people. After all, it makes great television, right?

Well, I don't know about you, but for me I don't get any form of pleasure from laying-off staff. It's one of the hardest things a CEO has to do. It never gets easier.

So, when should you hire more staff? I pondered this for a while and resorted to writing my own framework—a rational, systematic approach to a subject where we usually just 'go with our gut'.

In this chapter, I'll help you understand the If and When:

- If you should hire your next employee
- When you can afford to hire

More Employees Do Not Equal More Success

Next time you hear about a whiz bang, new 'fast growth' business in the media, pay attention to the numbers the founder or CEO is touting. If you listen closely, they will offer the following metrics to help you understand their 'success':

- How much money they raised
- Their revenue growth as a percentage, and
- Number of employees they have

In my personal view, raising money from investors is nothing to celebrate. I mean, you just gave up part of your company. I also don't remember the last time anyone made a song-and-dance because their bank loan was approved.

Secondly, revenue growth is not an indicator of a successful business. Enron had revenue in the hundreds of millions. Look where they ended up. Revenue is a vanity metric.

And so are employees. The number of employees you have in your business is not an indicator of a successful business. Actually, it can be the exact opposite.

More Headcount Does Not Produce More Leverage

I, too, was one of those 'grow at all costs' CEOs. In the early days of starting my company, I had a big and bold vision to disrupt my profession. More employees and more revenue would mean more success, right?

With bullish revenue growth projections, I recruited more people to service our customers. It worked when the business was growing. However, as soon as that revenue growth tapered, the hiring took longer to stop.

The result was we were left with excessive staff, not utilized to their full potential.

I needed to keep them busy and engaged, so I invented tasks for them to do—build processes, improve the operations. These were all value-add activities in my eyes, but not in theirs. My staff were doing work that wasn't a part of the position description.

They were confused about their place in the business. They lost trust. They thought I sold them a lie. And, although it wasn't intentional, in hindsight I did. I failed them, as a leader and as an employer.

The mistake I made? I hired too many people, too early.

It was a mutual decision to part ways with some of my staff, leaving a core group whom are still part of the business today. It was hard, but it was the right thing to do. I now have more time to spend with all my team members to lead and coach them. With less people comes less headaches.

The upside? Even with a smaller group, the same outcomes are being produced. As a team, we're working better together. As a leader, I am more effectively leveraging their abilities.

Want to Hire More Staff? Start Here

When you're stuck in the trenches, it's easy to assume that hiring more people is the solution to achieve the goals of your business. I mean, the more the better, right? Employees can add a great deal of value. But they also come with a lot of costs—both financial and mental.

So before assuming you need to hire more staff, ask yourself one simple question:

Do I need to?

When reviewing business functions you want to remove from your to-do list, consider this framework:

- Eliminate
- Automate
- Outsource

Eliminate: Using the 5 Why's

Taiichi Ohno was one of the inventors of the Toyota Production System—a lean management philosophy that is practiced across multiple industries, ranging from software to manufacturing. In his book, *Toyota Production System: Beyond Large-Scale Production*, Ohno describes a technique that is quintessential for problem solving referred to as 5 Why's.

When faced with a problem, our first reaction is to jump to a conclusion. A customer left you for a competitor? It's because the sales person oversold our value proposition. Why is everyone burning out? It's because we're too busy; we should hire more people.

As a species, we have a natural tendency to make judgment calls and react quickly. It served us well on the savanna, evading lions, but not so much in the modern day. That's where the 5 Why's come in. They can counter our own internal, unseen biases.

The process is simple. Just ask Why... five times.

Here's an example Toyota offers of how 5 Whys is used when an assembly line robot has failed.

1. *WHY* DID THE ROBOT STOP?

The circuit has overloaded, causing a fuse to blow.

2. *WHY* IS THE CIRCUIT OVERLOADED?

There just wasn't enough lubrication on the bearings, so they locked up.

3. *WHY* WAS THERE INSUFFICIENT LUBRICATION ON THE BEARINGS?

The oil pump on the robot is not circulating sufficient oil.

4. *WHY* IS THE PUMP NOT CIRCULATING SUFFICIENT OIL?

The pump intake is clogged with metal shavings.

5. *WHY* IS THE INTAKE CLOGGED WITH METAL SHAVINGS?

Because there is no filter on the pump.

If a manager decided that the robot was faulty, they could have justified the need to hire a team of electrical engineers to upgrade the robot circuit boards. Rather, the solution was a low-cost fix—easily handled by one of the existing team members.

Why are Customers Churning?

Here's how I've used the 5 Why's in my own business.

In Principle 2, I shared with you the customer churn challenges I faced early on. We were losing customers and were having trouble understanding why.

My business partner and I did a ton of research to understand the strategies and tactics we could implement to reduce churn. Everything we read about churn said that it was due to the onboarding process. Thus, we assumed the 'quick-fix' was to hire a dedicated customer success manager. This new person would be responsible for onboarding clients and ensuring they stay.

But the reality was that we couldn't afford to hire a full-time manager at the time. That financial constraint forced us to think about the underlying churn issue, and resolve it by other means.

Our deeper evaluation went something like this:

1. *WHY* ARE OUR CUSTOMERS CHURNING?

Because they are unhappy with our service.

2. *WHY* ARE THEY UNHAPPY WITH OUR SERVICE?

Because there's a misalignment of expectations.

3. *WHY* WAS THERE A MISALIGNMENT OF EXPECTATIONS?

Because we didn't scope our new customers properly at the engagement phase.

4. *WHY* DIDN'T WE SCOPE THEM PROPERLY DURING ENGAGEMENT?

Because we didn't qualify them to ensure they were the right customer for us.

5. *WHY* DIDN'T WE QUALIFY THEM BEFORE ENGAGING THEM?

Because we don't know who our target customer is.

We didn't have a churn problem because of poor onboarding. We had a churn problem because we were engaging the wrong customers in the first place. We had a sales qualifying problem. That's something we could fix which didn't involve hiring more people.

The 5 Why's is practiced by some of the world's smartest thinkers. It's akin to 'first principles thinking', a mental model famously used by Elon Musk. Actively questioning everything you think you know helps to reframe problems. This can lead to innovative solutions.

Solutions (that sometimes) don't require hiring people to solve.

Automate

"The first rule of any technology used in a business is that automation applied to an efficient operation will magnify the efficiency. The second is that automation applied to an inefficient operation will magnify the inefficiency."

Bill Gates

You can get obsessive with automating the crap out of business processes, and you should. Automation is the key to leverage.

Here are some rules when it comes to automation:

- Never automate something that can be eliminated
- Never attempt to automate something without building and designing a process for it
- If a task or workflow is repeated more than three times by a human, automate it

You don't need to be a software developer to automate stuff. Tools like Zapier are built for non-tech people (like myself) and can help you automate tasks and push data between software. I've included a list of tools to help you at the end of this Principle.

Outsource

"Because the purpose of business is to create a customer, the business enterprise has two—and only two—basic functions: marketing and innovation."

Peter Drucker

Amazon's mission is to be 'the world's most customer-centric company.' The competencies that they need to achieve this mission are customer experience, leveraging data, and technology.

Apple's core competencies are simplicity through design and technology. They deliver a suite of products which are uniquely Apple—functional, innovative, and beautiful.

Every business has a core set of competencies that define its uniqueness and its competitive advantage. It's this relentless focus on these competencies that makes a business unique and valuable.

When it comes to building a long-term enterprise, you as the founder should focus on your unique value proposition. Any task or function that does not align to this should be outsourced.

If you have less than 30 staff, the employees that you hire should grow your unique competencies, and grow your revenue.

Otherwise, outsource it. Any task that is non-revenue producing and non-core to your business can be done by someone else. Examples of these functions include:

- Accounting and bookkeeping
- Payroll
- Email management
- Administration
- Social media
- Human resources
- Recruitment
- Editing content

There's an entire economy built on the premise of outsourcing random business tasks. Platforms like Upwork and Fiverr are marketplaces for freelancers from around the world to help you manage odd jobs. So, take the non-essential off your plate.

When Can I Afford to Hire a New Staff Member?

Okay, now that you've decided you *do* need to hire a staff member —and you have essential work for them to do—let's see how to get a grip on if you can actually *afford* to hire that person.

But, before we begin, a quick disclaimer.

This guide is for small businesses that are growing within some form of financial constraint. That is, you don't have a bottomless pit of investor's money. If you are a funded tech startup, the same principles will still apply. However, they are less applicable for founders in early revenue ventures that predominantly hire developers and product teams. Let's begin.

Rule 1: Forecasted Sales of at Least 2x Monthly Salary

Employees are assets. They may not be accounted for on your balance sheet, but they do add financial value to your business. If you let them.

Employees need time get up and running. They're not machines that are instantly productive with the flick of a switch. They need time to adjust into their role. The costs of time, as well as the resources and energy to get there, put constraints on your business.

The effort that your team spends training new hires could otherwise be spent generating revenue. The result is the costs of new hires can outweigh your revenue growth. This can lead to little or no profit. Or, in the worst-case scenario, create losses.

It's important that you factor in enough revenue to not only cover the direct cost of the new employee (salary and benefits), but the indirect costs of training and ramp-up time as well.

So what's enough revenue? You want to set aside at least two times the new hire's monthly salary cost with secured (brand new) revenue in the same month the new person is hired. This revenue allows a buffer to cover the costs, plus some.

For example, if your new hire has a salary of $6K per month, you should have at least $12K of new committed sales. This revenue should be sold before signing any employment contract.

The Waves of Hiring

The risk posed by not having enough revenue to support the cost of your new hires is that you 'erode' your profit—meaning that the costs incurred by employing each staff member outweigh any new sales generated. If this hiring cycle continues, you run the risk of growing revenue and gaining employees with no actual profit.

You run the risk of creating a bloated inefficient business—an enormous, growing beast that swallows its own tail.

The diagram on the next page shows a business that hires its new team members on 'gut feel'. Every time sales grow, the business hires an additional team member to service those new customers.

Maybe this sounds okay, but the problem is that the profit generated from these new sales is eroded by the new staff member's salary, the one servicing the new customers. To stop this crazy cycle from continuing, you have to figure out your hiring economics.

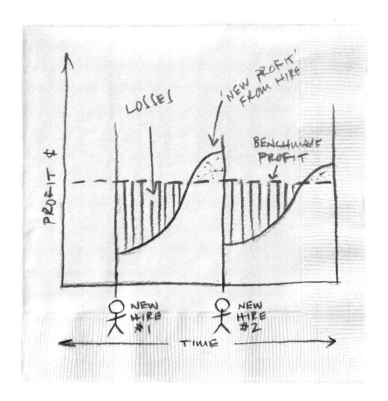

Having new revenue at least 2x the employee cost ensures that your business remains profitable with new hires. The result is that you grow revenue, headcount, and profit—all at the same time.

The way that most businesses hire is visually scribbled on the napkin above. In this example, every time a new employee is hired, the salary costs erode any profit earned from new sales. The company continues to make more sales to the extent the employee's costs are covered. Eventually, they will reach a point where finally some of that new revenue converts into new profit.

But that's until the business hires again. Then, the costs of the new hire will again eat into new profit. It's a self-perpetuating cycle.

From an outsiders view, the business appears to be crushing it, as it's growing revenue and headcount. The problem is that it's all vanity, because underneath the hood they're rarely converting that growth into new profit. They're growing revenue and costs, but not profit. It's a vicious cycle.

By contrast, the napkin sketch below shows a business that hires under the 2x New Revenue Model. As you can see, the business is maintaining profitability as they employ new staff. This is because there's enough new revenue (plus some) to carry the costs of the new hire until that person ramps up. This business is not just maintaining profitability, it's actually increasing it as well.

This is the type of healthy growth you should be striving for as a business owner. The hiring methodology under 2x Revenue Model will help you grow revenue, headcount, and profit. Growth and profitability is not a trade-off. You can have both.

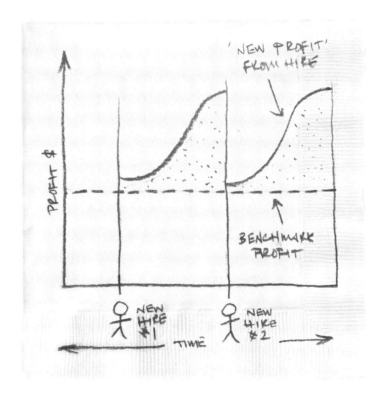

What about Non-Revenue Generating Support Staff?

So far my hiring methodology applies to revenue-generating team members, like technicians responsible for delivering your product or service. For example, Brendan's team of creative staff that are doing billable work. But what about non-revenue-generating folks, like your operations manager or administrative roles?

How does the 2x Model apply to these support staff, as they don't have a direct role in producing revenue?

This is a common misconception. All of your support staff play a role in the bigger picture. Don't forget, they are there to support the people responsible for revenue-producing work. Their role takes away some of the 'non-revenue-producing tasks' so that the revenue-producing folks can do their best work.

The 2x Revenue metric is still applicable for these employees, because any non-revenue producing employee should help to improve the leverage and productivity of revenue-producing ones.

What about Sales and Customer Success Employees?

Sales people and customer success roles are categorized as 'Customer Acquisition Costs' from a financial perspective. Their role in the business is to bring in the new revenue, rather than to support and service existing customers.

We covered the economics of hiring these roles back in Chapter 10. For these folks, it's about the Customer Lifetime Value equation.

What If I'm Busting at the Seams with Revenue?

Back in the day—when it came to hiring new staff—the gauge I used was how busy we were. If the team was up to their elbows with work and we were busting at the seams, it was time to hire another person. We're all busy; that means there's room to grow, right?

Being 'busy' doesn't mean you are being effective or productive. For example, your business could be delivering its product inefficiently, or burning too much time doing back-office admin.

In this case, hiring more people will not fix any of your underlying productivity issues. It will result in more headaches, more costs, and less profit.

If you feel the need to hire more staff and the 2x Model of new committed revenue is not there to support any new hires, there's a bigger problem with your business.

That's worth restating: If you 'need' to hire before you can afford it, you have a different problem.

Maybe you're not pricing your product or service correctly. Or it could be that you're producing what you sell inefficiently. Remember, if you hire before you're ready, you'll only magnify whatever your true issue is. It's okay; don't stress out.

You can understand where the problem resides by calculating your revenue per employee metric. If it's below the benchmark you need—improve that metric first. Figure out what tweaks you can make in your business to increase the leverage of your staff.

Rule 2: Always Have 2 Months Wages in Cash

The difficulty with 'making payroll' is often due to late paying customers. Although your company might be profitable, the cash may not be available in your bank account. To protect yourself from this issue, have 2 months of your new employee's payroll set aside in cash before you hire them.

Having this cash available on-hand protects you from 60-day accounts receivables.

Remember, it's unlikely that your new hire will be revenue and cash flow-generating from day one. Having a buffer of cash in the bank protects you.

As business owners we can get caught up in the adrenaline of growth and expansion. Before you jump to conclusions on hiring staff, ask yourself: Do I actually need more people? And, secondly, can I really afford them?

Bigger doesn't mean better.

Principle 4 Takeaways

- Your company's most important asset isn't stuff. It's your people. Building a business is about leverage. You should focus on maximizing the leverage of your team.

- Measure the leverage of your employees using the Revenue per Employee metric. It's calculated as Total Revenue divided by the Total Number of Employees.

- Timesheets can suck. But having them implemented in your business—and having buy-in from all your employess—can help you find new opportunities to increase your leverage.

- Here are a few tactics on how to make timesheets *not* suck:

   ° Educate your team on why they're being implemented
   ° Don't require time to be kept in tiny blocks
   ° Let your team in on the process; review data as a group

- Within your business, more employees do not equal more success. Before hiring anyone, ask yourself: Do you even need to? Consider this framework:

   ° Eliminate
   ° Automate
   ° Outsource

- If you're convinced you need to hire, calculate if you can afford to. The two rules are:

   ° Have forecasted sales for 2x the new hire's monthly salary
   ° Always have 2 months of their salary as cash in the bank

SOFTWARE TOOLS FOR PRINCIPLE 4

Below are some timesheet tools that you can explore to find the right fit for your organization:

- Harvest: www.getharvest.com

- TSheets: www.tsheets.com

- Toggl: www.toggl.com

Principle 5

SHARPEN THE SAW

DEVELOPING GOOD HABITS

Achieving any goal is the accumulation of good habits that you practice daily. In this section, I give you my recipe book to transform your business—using your numbers.

"Begin with the end in mind."

Stephen Covey

LOSS AVERSION BUDGETING

Don't Go With Your Gut

Ah… the beginning of a new financial year.

The clock resets, as does your year-to-date Profit & Loss. It's a good time to start afresh, setting new goals for the next arduous 12 months of the small business grind.

It's around this time when Bob the CPA tells you to update your budget. Remember that? The 5-page document you paid him about $3K for a year ago? It's somewhere in that bottom drawer.

If you're like most business owners, you haven't looked at that budget since it was developed. Perhaps you don't even have one. I'm guilty of that, too. I actually despise the budget-setting process.

It always involves a painful discussion-slash-workshop with your accountant where you examine a lot of trivial details like your projected expenses for the coming 12 months. A lot of minutiae.

When you do try to measure your actual performance against the budget, usually it's way over because you didn't project enough repairs and maintenance expenses for that broken-down truck, or the recruitment fees to replace the staff member who decided to go MIA. But, realistically, how could you have predicted that?

Let's be honest, budgets are almost useless because you have no idea what will happen next month—let alone next year.

A lot of work for not much gain.

Despite budgets being a pain in the butt, they do have their uses. The value is not the PDF or Excel spreadsheet. It's in the process. It can help you and your team quantify your company's goals into an accountability framework. It gets you thinking about how you will practically achieve those objectives by getting granular with your core business drivers.

For example, rather than setting a goal of 'growing revenue by 10%', building a budget makes you think about *how* you will grow the additional revenue. How many leads you need to generate? At what average sale value? And at what conversion rate?

By digging into the details, you start to manage and measure activity. This allows you and your team to augment your decision-making with data, rather than just 'going with your gut'.

In addition to the long-term strategic value of having a budget, the immediate benefit is the ability to forecast your future cash and financial position. By assessing projected sales, expenses, and cash flow, it allows you to make proactive decisions.

For example, if your sales are expected drop off a cliff due to the holiday season, having a process to understand the impact to cash flow can help you mitigate these type of issues in advance. You can prepare for it, perhaps by getting access to a line of credit.

In summary, a budget can help you be prepared.

But, as I mentioned at the top, it can also be limiting.

On Breaking-Even

In the early stages of starting my business, I knew I'd be racking up losses. No big deal. Every business takes time to ramp up and be profitable, right?

I 'borrowed' some cash from my personal savings to fund the losses that would be incurred in the first few months of trading.

Despite having little revenue, budgeting for the company's monthly expenses was pretty simple. I had a good handle on what the outgoing, recurring expenses were each month. While my business was simple in those days, it was also stressful. My Profit & Loss was continually in the red. I was burning money.

Even though I had the cash to fund these losses, I couldn't help but cringe every time I saw that monthly P&L.

I hate the idea of waste and inefficiency, and looking at my business from a financial lens, I was literally throwing away money. Mentally, it hurt—a lot. I should have just dumped all that cash into a bin and set it on fire, because that's basically what I was doing.

After several months I realized it wasn't helpful beating myself up about it. Instead, I started to channel that pain and focus. My goal was to get to break-even... by selling more.

Okay, I think you've already realized that I am not a 'sales guy'. I've been a technically-trained accountant my whole life, so my sales journey had a steep learning curve. But I made it work.

It was a daily battle—getting up every morning, prospecting, and facing rejection after rejection. You win a few; you lose a few. Then, finally, the wins outnumber the losses.

I still remember the feeling when my business went from red to black. Pure relief. Mind you, there was still plenty of road ahead. We were 'profitable' at a ramen-eating level, but not if you adjusted for a market value salary.

My feeling of relief was driven more by the fact that we were no longer losing money. I reached my first goal: we were at break-even. The pressure was suddenly off. I could sleep better at night. The world was back in equilibrium.

For a couple of months I took my foot off the gas, slowed down on the push to prospect for new business. As a result, our sales started to flatline, even plateau.

We still weren't 'profitable', but we weren't losing money either. I was in this comfortable, but weird, place where just doing 'enough' was okay. It was starting to gnaw at me.

The strangest thing was that, yeah, we were profitable, but that didn't make me any happier. Well, nowhere near as happy as the moment we moved from losing money to making money.

Turns out, this is a cognitive bias that humans possess known as Loss Aversion.

Losses are More Powerful than Gains

Imagine you're walking to the bus stop and see a $100 bill on the pavement. You take a look around to see if anyone is watching, then snatch it—shoving it into your back pocket or purse. How do you feel? Pretty lucky, right?

Still on a high from your recent win, you decide to indulge in a bit of retail therapy. You head to the department store on your lunch break to buy a new jacket. It's on sale for $99. Perfect.

After trying it on, you skip over to the register to pay. You open your wallet and are shocked to find that the $100 is missing. WTF!

You panic, get angry. You're frustrated with yourself: 'How did I manage to lose a $100 in less than four hours?' You reach into your pockets and pat your thighs, but you come up empty. All the while the cashier glares at you with a weird, judgmental look.

You're embarrassed and pissed—not only because you can't get the jacket, but because you've lost a chunk of your money.

Practically, you're not better or worse from a net cash position, because that $100 was a bonus you happened to find. But, the feeling of *losing* that surprise money was greater than the feeling of *finding* it in the first place.

This is an example of loss aversion bias, which psychologists use to describe people's tendency to prefer avoiding losses as opposed to acquiring equivalent gains. In other words, it's better to *not* lose $100 than it is to *gain* $100.

Loss aversion is a powerful bias with studies suggesting that the pain of losing something is twice as much as the pleasure of gaining exactly the same item.

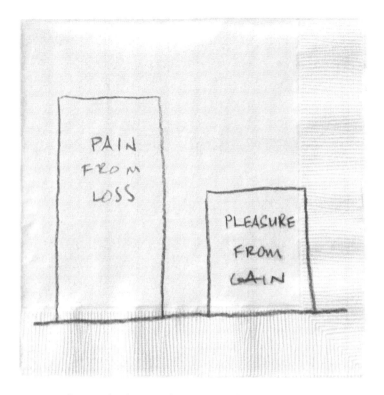

Now flipping back to my business profit situation, the feeling of making profit was nowhere near as powerful as not losing money. I relied upon that sense of anger, fear, and urgency to drive my performance to stop losing money. But, now that it was gone, where was the 'inner me' to kick me in the butt?

Loss aversion explains why threats typically take precedence over opportunities when it comes to our own personal motivation. The threat of loss often requires our immediate attention because, quite often, they are extremely costly—or even life-threatening. It's hardwired into our DNA.

Think about it from an evolutionary perspective. Losing a loved one to a saber-toothed tiger, or facing starvation from a bad harvest is a horrible experience. We're built to do everything in our power to prevent that from happening.

In my case, it was the potential of losing my business. I poured every ounce of energy into ensuring its survival. But once I got there, then what? Well, I barely survived. I eked out a living.

Without some form of accountability system, I'm probably the laziest human to walk the earth. Just ask my dog Bella; she loves to walk the earth (specifically every day). No matter what the weather —rain, hail, or shine—she's waiting for me impatiently at the front door. As a side note, I truly admire the motivation of dogs.

However my own lack of get-up-and-go really sucks, because it's up to me to drive our company performance, to set an example. And, obviously, there's a lot at stake.

Since the feeling of 'gaining' was nowhere near as powerful, in my mind, as the equivalent losses, I reframed the situation.

On Goal Setting

As a business owner, every strategic decision you make is always 'gain' orientated. You probably started a business in order to work for yourself. When you hire a certain employee it might be so you can focus more on leading your staff. Both are examples of gains.

The challenge with constantly making decisions which are driven by gains is that the process can start to lose its shine after a while. The feeling of gaining isn't quite as powerful as the feeling of not losing.

We've all heard the stories of once-successful businesses that lose their mojo because they get complacent.

Success, in this instance, can be a curse.

It often takes some form of a crisis to pull the company together and return to a growth mindset: a new competitor, a disruptive technology, a global financial crisis.

For example, a number of the world's greatest companies were spawned from some type of catastrophe. General Electric, IBM, General Motors, and Disney all started during a depression.

It takes exceptional leadership to drive innovation in crisis, and if executed well, the business can pull together. People are inspired to change, to move more quickly—the reality of losing their jobs is enough of a threat to unite everyone to fix problems as a team.

The thing is, waiting for a 'crisis' to drive action and growth is a terrible strategy. I would rather be the leader that drives change, not waiting for an event to change me.

The problem is, I'm lazy.

As a serial procrastinator thrown into the deep end of being a leader of my company, the buck stops with me. I'm responsible for the growth, longevity, and prosperity of my business, and also the well-being of my employees and customers. Laziness, then, is a non-winning posture for me to carry.

So how does a business get its act together? How do you continually inspire your people to change, to move more quickly? How can you harness the feeling of loss aversion without acting like every day in the office is a three-alarm fire?

I've experimented with different ways to deal with this. Rather than waiting for a 'crisis' to drive action and growth, I discovered a new way to do goal setting that 'flips the script' on loss aversion. I do it by reframing opportunity costs.

Opportunity Costs

Opportunity cost is the value of a lost opportunity; the benefit of the thing you could have done instead of what you're doing now.

Typically applied in the field of finance and economics, the opportunity cost concept is generally only considered in financial investment opportunities.

For example, if I invest in shares at a 10% yield, what is the opportunity cost if I invest that same money into my business to generate more profit?

The problem is most people don't consider the actual costs of day-to-day decisions. Opportunity cost is at its most expensive when we *miss* opportunities.

Think of the cost of not investing in training that new employee. Of not listening to a new idea. Of not investing in that new product. These opportunities are significant, and we overlook them all the time.

You know what's even worse? The opportunity cost of inaction keeps rising.

In strategic projects, the benefits are always 'gain' orientated. When you develop a new product, it opens opportunities to take market share. If you open a new office, it might expand your global footprint. Indeed, for many important decisions, your company will be better off by doing them. But being 'better-off' isn't a strong enough incentive… Well, for me anyway.

I've found it personally helpful to re-frame goals—not viewing them as opportunity gains I can potentially realize by *achieving* them, but rather by the opportunity cost of *not* doing them.

The cost of not growing, of not being remarkable, of not helping my team be the best versions of themselves far outweighs the gains of simply being 'better'.

I regularly apply this in my personal life, as well, but the most profound impact it's had has been on my business. In fact, it's now imbedded into our strategic planning process.

Our process begins with identifying and quantifying all the possible opportunity costs. We build them into our financial and strategic business goals.

Cue Loss Aversion Budgeting

During the next strategy session with my business partner, we talked about what our collective financial goals were. What did we actually desire to achieve with our business?

We asked ourselves the following questions:

- What salary, beyond our MVL, would we actually be happy with? Meaning the next step up, an above average situation.

- How much in dividends did we want our business to produce every year? Meaning our financial return, adjusted for the risk, sweat, and the financial capital we had invested.

- Aspirationally, what would we like to sell our business for? (It was a bit early for this maybe, but it's good to talk about.)

Believe me, we went deep; it got personal. And I mean that in the best way possible. It was a meaningful discussion. We came out on the other end with a clear sense of our financial goals.

They went something like this:

- Pay ourselves a $150K annual salary by end of the year
- Build the business to generate a $1M EBIT margin per year
- Work only 20 hours a week in the business
- Sell the business in 5 years for $20M

These were our opportunity cost targets.

Of course, it would take time (and effort) to achieve all of those objectives, so we had to start small. We began by focusing on our first objective—increasing each of our salaries.

At this stage the company had enough of a history that we could reliably predict the future. Thus, knowing our actual fixed monthly costs, we simply added in the 'additional wage' we wanted to pay ourselves beyond the MVLs we'd begun the company with. This set a new 'opportunity cost' benchmark.

We then reverse-engineered the amount of new sales we needed to make in order to meet our higher target 'break-even'.

Of course, with more sales comes more customers. And more customers means more staff and associated costs required to service those new customers. As part of our budgeting process, we also had to consider everything that would go along with generating that new revenue.

By notionally reflecting the target financial goal as an 'expense' in our budget, it set a new benchmark for what the business had to achieve as a minimum to break-even on our goals. Anything below our 'opportunity cost' benchmark was framed as a 'loss' in our minds, which drove our ambition to level up as a business.

Our Profit & Loss was once again in the 'red'—a self-created red. The objective was to avert these 'losses' and do whatever it took to get it back into the 'black'. The pressure was back on.

Loss aversion budgeting is a tool that we continue to use to this day. You can build one for yourself. Here's how:

How to Create a Loss Aversion Budget

What's the one thing everybody knows about keeping control of their finances, whether it's a personal checking account or a huge business? Make more money than you spend. Plain and simple.

In traditional accounting, it's expressed in the equation:

$$SALES - EXPENSES = PROFIT$$

However, loss aversion budgeting requires you to reframe this equation. Rather than starting with sales, you should begin with your expenses, then add your quantified 'opportunity costs':

$$ACTUAL\ EXPENSES + OPPORTUNITY\ COSTS =$$
$$TARGET\ SALES\ REQUIRED\ TO\ BREAK\text{-}EVEN$$

This value sets the basis of the total costs—from both the actual and 'opportunity' side—that you need to cover before profit starts.

Let's look at the steps for how to create a loss aversion budget:

- Define your 'opportunity costs'
- Calculate your fixed recurring expenses
- Understand the variable expenses as a percentage of revenue
- Add your 'opportunity costs'
- Calculate the sales needed to 'break-even' on your total costs

STEP 1 - DEFINE YOUR OPPORTUNITY COST

Ultimately, your financial goals depend on the phase of your business machine, and what you want to achieve from it.

Common examples of financial goals include:

- Break-even in 6 months
- Pay all the founders market salaries by X months
- Give all employees a 10% pay raise by X date
- Pay a dividend of X by X date
- Work less than 4 hours a week on the business by X date

Ensure you are specific about the $ value and timeframe that you want to achieve for each goal. Don't worry yet about whether they are realistic. We will 'stress test' these numbers shortly.

Now that you've got your goals defined, quantify each one into an expense.

For example, if your goal is to pay yourself an additional $70K salary per annum, your opportunity cost is $70K per annum.

If your goal is to work less than 4 hours a week on the business or 'make yourself redundant', calculate how many staff you will need to employ to do the roles you play in the business, and calculate the monthly wages of those employees.

Opportunity Cost Goal	Quantified Goal (in $)
Give the founders a pay raise to $120K per annum, from $50K by the end of the year	$70K opportunity cost per annum, per founder
Give all employees a 10% pay raise, the equivalent to $500K by end of the year	$500K of opportunity cost, per annum
Pay a dividend of $1M per annum	$1M of opportunity cost, per annum

There are no rules on what opportunity cost goals you set. The key is to be aspirational about your objectives. Whatever the result, try your best to quantify it back into dollar terms so you can build it into your budget, and know what your business needs generate to achieve those ends. Remember, your business is your machine; you must engineer it to generate the outcomes that you desire.

STEP 2 - CALCULATE YOUR MONTHLY RECURRING FIXED EXPENSES

Traditional budgeting fails most businesses because, in the real world, it's impossible to predict what your expenses will be next month, let alone in six or thirty-six.

Instead of wasting your time predicting the future, this process focuses on the things that you can control and have certainty over. Let's start with your Monthly Recurring Expenses (MRE).

For this exercise, go and review your most recent Profit & Loss statement. Identify (maybe with a yellow highlighter) all the costs that recur, no matter what sales or revenue your business generates. The most common examples of this include:

- Rent
- Utilities
- Insurance
- Wages
- Your salary

STEP 3 – CALCULATE VARIABLES AS A PERCENTAGE OF REVENUE

If you have an inventory-based business like Sarah at Moo Formula, your variable expenses should be fairly predictable, so you want to calculate them as a percentage of revenue. Thus we can forecast these expenses as being directly correlated to revenue.

STEP 4 – ADD RECURRING COSTS TO OPPORTUNITY COSTS

Now that you have quanitifed both your actual recurring fixed expenses and your opportunity costs, add them together. This forms the total fixed costs required to arrive at break-even on your opportunity cost goals.

STEP 5 – CALCULATE BREAK-EVEN SALES ON TOTAL COSTS

Now that you have your total recurring and opportunity costs, calculate the sales required to hit the break-even point on these total costs. The break-even sales formula is:

(ACTUAL EXPENSES + OPPORTUNITY COSTS)
/ CONTRIBUTION MARGIN

Let's use a practical example:

Example: Brendan's Goals for Voltage Media

Recall my chat with Brendan at the pub. You might remember he was overworked, stuck as a cog in his machine. Due to all the hours he was working in his business, he was suffering personally.

GOAL 1 – INCREASE ANNUAL SALARY

Also, at the moment, Brendan has been drawing a humble wage of $60K per annum. He'd like to give himself a pay raise so he and his family can live a more comfortable personal life. He's thinking something more like $180K per annum. A hefty increase.

GOAL 2 – DECREASE AMOUNT OF HOURS WORKED

We decided that Brendan needed support at a management level to help him take care of the 'fire fighting'. An extra set of hands would help him work less hours and also free him up to focus on higher level activities. Employing a General Manager would cost $150K per annum in salary, inclusive of benefits.

Let's quantify what his opportunity costs look like. In total, Brendan will incur an additional $270K of opportunity costs to achieve his business goal of working less hours and a higher salary.

Remember that Voltage Media is a services-based business, so most of its expenses are fixed costs—like wages and office rent. Irrespective of how much revenue the company brings in, these costs will always be there month-on-month.

Opportunity Costs Quantification
Voltage Media LLC

Opportunity	Annual Cost
Pay raise to $180k	$120,000
General Manager (salary)	$150,000
	$270,000

In Brendan's case, the total recurring expenses are $2.1M per annum. Voltage Media also has a low amount of variable expenses. In his industry the average is about 10%.

Take your total recurring costs and add the opportunity costs.

Total Opportunity Costs Calculation
Voltage Media LLC

Annual Recurring expenses	$2,100,000
Add: Opportunity Costs	
Opportunity Cost - Payrise to $180k p.a	$120,000
Opportunity Cost - General Manager	$150,000
	$270,000
Total Annual Recurring Expenses	**$2,370,000**

This means that Voltage Media will incur $2.37M of annual fixed expenses from an actual and opportunity cost level.

Now, let's calculate the sales that Brendan needs to generate in order to break-even on the opportunity cost he's chosen.

OPPORTUNITY COST BREAK-EVEN =
FIXED RECURRING EXPENSES / CONTRIBUTION MARGIN

Break-even = $2,370,000 / 90%
Break-even sales per annum = $2,633,334

Voltage Media needs to generate $2.63M of annual sales to reach opportunity cost break-even.

Total Opportunity Cost Break-even Sales Target
Voltage Media LLC

Annual Recurring expenses	$2,100,000
Add: Opportunity Costs	
Opportunity Cost - Payrise to $180k p.a	$120,000
Opportunity Cost - General Manager	$150,000
	$270,000
Total annual recurring expenses	**$2,370,000**
Contribution Margin	90%
Opportunity Cost Break-even sales target	**$2,633,333**

Budgeting for your Sales

Ugh... So Brendan needs to do $2.63M of sales to hit his goal?

Eyeing a high break-even for target sales often gives founders a humble dose of 'Holy crap, how the hell are we supposed to reach that?' This is normal. Your opportunity cost goals should scare you. If you're not setting stretch targets, you are settling for average.

Like achieving any goal, the key is to break it up into bite-sized chunks. You've set the macro goals, now it's time to set the micro, starting with your revenue.

STEP 1 - UNDERSTAND YOUR RECURRING REVENUE

The majority of businesses will have multiple revenue streams. Most commonly, these revenue streams are comprised of sales from different types of products and services.

The key to understanding the future is predictability—knowing which of these sales are recurring in nature or not.

The term 'recurring revenue' includes all income that's recurring in nature—for example, subscription sales, managed services, and retainer-based contracts. Recurring revenue is the holy grail and you should consider ways to maximize this in your business.

Non-recurring revenue includes income which is one-off in nature. This is comprised mostly of project work—projects that you do for customers which are unlikely to occur again.

Similarly to what we did with expenses, you should analyze your business activity to understand your monthly recurring revenue. Don't pay any attention to non-recurring, or project revenue, for the moment. We don't want to forecast for stuff that we don't have any certainty over.

In the Voltage Media example, approximately 65% of revenue is contracted, retainer-based work. That means of the total $2.4M of sales the company did in the previous financial year, Brendan has comfort that $1.56M (65%) will reoccur in this year. That's revenue that we can bank on in our Loss Aversion Budget.

Opportunity Cost Profit/(Loss) Calculation
Voltage Media LLC

Opportunity Cost Break-even Sales Target	$2,633,333
Annual Recurring Revenue	$1,560,000
Opportunity Cost Profit/(Loss)	**($1,073,333)**

Notice how the gap is lower as we've already got some certainty over the revenue. Now we just need to make up the shortfall.

STEP 2 - SPLIT THE REVENUE SHORTFALL IN BITE-SIZED CHUNKS

Looking at your budget from an annual basis is overwhelming and simply not practical.

What we want to do is split up your sales targets into months or quarters, then think about what activities you and your sales team need to be doing on a micro-basis to achieve those targets.

For example, get granular with your revenue equation (refer to the discussion in Principle 2). Calculate the number of leads and conversion rate and backsolve what activity you need to do in order to acheive those new sales.

Take it a step further by converting the sales $ into units. For example, how many customers at what average sales price do you need to close to generate that revenue?

The more specific you can be with your micro-goals, the more focused you and your team can be on achieving them.

Using Voltage Media as an example, your final Loss Aversion Budget should look something like this.

Loss Aversion Budget for the year ended 31 December 2018
Voltage Media LLC

	31-Mar-2018	30-Jun-2018	30-Sep-2018	31-Dec-2018
Total Recurring Expenses	$592,500	$592,500	$592,500	$592,500
Opportunity Cost Break-even Sales Target	$658,333	$658,333	$658,333	$658,333
Recurring Revenue	$390,000	$390,000	$390,000	$390,000
Opportunity Cost Profit/(Loss)	**($268,333)**	**($268,333)**	**($268,333)**	**($268,333)**

Your goal is to avoid the losses, and get to break-even.

Final Remarks

Business, like life, is an infinite game. There is no definable 'end'. You continue to grind and push forward, no matter what hurdle or obstacle you face.

With persistent effort, you will achieve your goals, and you should celebrate these wins. The challenge you face is that the feeling of winning will diminish over time.

Rather than relying on will power and ambition for achieving your goals, reframe what it means to *not* achieve them.

Instead of winning, focus on 'not losing'.

Accounting is often criticized as being solely about the past, a quantification of what's already occurred. But, in fact, 'stark naked' accounting is a tool of high leverage in the here and now.

I hope you're seeing that the principles within this book, while rooted in the truth of the past, help you accurately predict which branches of your business will bear fruit tomorrow. This insight into the future can help you make better decisions today.

"Give me six hours to chop down a tree, and I will spend the first four sharpening the axe."

Abraham Lincoln

MY RECIPE BOOK
FOR NUMBERS

The 'One Thing' About Pizza

Italian immigrant Pasquale Giammarco started his business for a reason similar to yours or mine: dissatisfaction with the status quo.

Pat's pain point was American pizzas. The pizzas weren't up to scratch: cheap processed ham, plastic cheese, and thick heavy dough that gave most patrons heartburn. For a native Italian, American pizzas were an insult. In 1978, he founded Marco's Pizza —an authentic, high-quality pizzaria using artisan ingredients—in order to make a pie worthy of his heritage.

Today, the Marco's Pizza franchise has over $345 million in annual sales as a group with over 800 stores across the United States, the Bahamas, and even India. It still remains the only pizza chain started by a native Italian. Like all great businesses, Marco's Pizza paid strict attention to the numbers.

The CFO of Marco's Pizza, Ken Switzer, saw the privately-held chain of pizza restaurants grow from 30 stores to over 600 during his 27-year tenure with the company.

What does he credit the company's success to? Their relentless focus on reducing staff turnover.

Marco's has found that the one thing critical to their financial performance and growth is fostering employee satisfaction. In an interview with the *Wall Street Journal*, Switzer said this:

> *"Turnover is the statistic we measure, but that's really a reflection of employee engagement… The average turnover in quick service industries is around 100%… We know that we can improve profitability by 1.8 percent, when you lower turnover from 100% to 50%."*

Focusing on one thing has been critical to their success.

A 'One Thing' About Renting Out Your Bedroom

The year was 2007. College friends Bryan Chesky and Joe Gebbina were both 27-year-old design students, struggling to pay rent for their apartment in downtown San Francisco.

There was a design conference coming to town and all the city hotels were booked up. Their idea? Pull out an air mattress and turn their apartment into a bed-and-breakfast. Jumping on this opportunity to earn a few extra dollars to make rent, they hacked together a website and brought total strangers into their home.

In 2008, Airbnb was accepted into Y Combinator, the famed startup incubator, where they received seed money and access to world-class mentors to get the company off the ground.

But it wasn't an instant success. With sluggish bookings, the team poured over their listings with Paul Graham (the founder of Y Combinator) to understand why nothing was sticking. After hours of review, they made an interesting observation:

> *"We noticed a pattern… that the photos sucked. People were using their camera phones or using their images from classified sites. It actually wasn't a surprise that people weren't booking rooms, because you couldn't even really see what it is that you were paying for."*

To follow-up on this insight, the team booked a flight to New York to spend time with their customers. They rented a camera and replaced the amateur images with high-resolution, professional photos. The founders were testing a simple hypothesis: hosts with professional photography get more business.

Just weeks later, the results were in: weekly revenue doubled. They knew they were onto something.

In mid-2011, they sent 20 photographers to take pictures of host houses. The effect of posting these attractive images was so positive that by 2012 Airbnb was doing 5,000 shoots per month. The founders maintain this strategy was fundamental to their success.

Focusing their attention and efforts on one single metric—hosts with professional photography do better—propelled the company.

What's Your One Thing?

In a world where we can literally quantify everything, numbers and data can be overwhelming.

The thing is, generating and collecting this data is not the problem. The hard part is deciding which numbers are actually relevant to your business goals.

In other words, what's the One Thing critical to your success?

Accountants call this metric an economic driver. It's the one key metric in your business that everyone in your team can understand and get behind. If it's moving in the right direction, your business performance will, too.

The relentless focus on this One Thing is a very simple and powerful tool to drive your company's performance, because it gives you focus. It helps you narrow your decision-making process to understand how your strategy will impact that single number.

Sometimes your One Thing is obvious. In the case of Marco's Pizza, it seems like common sense that the single focus on reducing employee turnover would improve profitability. Employees are assets, and the longer we can keep them engaged and retained in the business, the more value they can create.

In a business like Moo Formula, for example, Sarah's One Thing could be the number of repeating customers. Repeat customers is a metric that is easily understood by the team, and directly correlated to the success of her business. For Moo Formula, the more repeat customers they have, the higher the customer lifetime value. And that converts to more revenue.

But what about Airbnb? Correlating the quality of photography to the number of bookings is not a metric that jumps out at you. I mean, in hindsight it makes sense. It's hard for people to know what they're renting if they can't see it. But, at first glance, you couldn't guess that 'quality photography' was the key metric to their success. You could almost say it was a fluke that they were able to find that.

While we'd all like to discover an obscure and miracle metric in our business that can make us instant billionaires, I'm a realist. Also, I don't have the patience to scour through our webpage data looking for trends that are probably just noise. Rather, let's go back to the Pareto Principle.

In this chapter, I share the 20% of numbers that will give you 80% of the leverage to drive a better, more profitable business.

"Lies, Damned Lies, and Statistics"

Mark Twain popularized this saying, and many entrepreneurs feel the same about tracking KPIs as a form of management. It's all lies, damned lies, and statistics. Just more corporate BS.

At the start of this book, I asserted that entrepreneurs are liars. We deceive ourselves all the time. But, as you can see, numbers can lie, too. Numbers and data are not always perfect and don't always provide you with the full picture.

In order to understand the real story behind your numbers, they have to be interpreted and presented in context. Looking too intently at one metric can take you down the wrong path.

My assertion is that numbers provide us with objectivity and tell a version of the truth. The flaw, however, is that they can be taken out of context far too easily.

Want me to prove it? Take a look at the example below of a company who's year-on-year growth rate is plummeting.

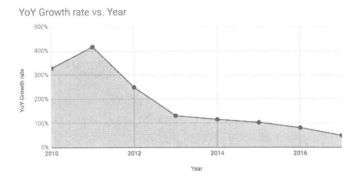

The company has had amazing YoY growth in its early years. However since 2011, its growth rates have slowed rapidly, heading towards zero. Taken in the context of 'slowing growth', one could say that this company is failing. But… And it's a big 'but'…

The data displayed above measures the guest numbers using Airbnb's platform, as publicly tweeted by Brian Chesky.

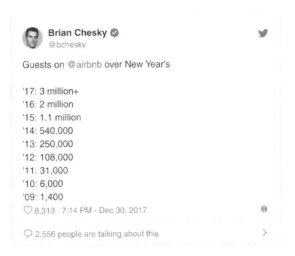

At the time I'm writing, Airbnb has a valuation of $31 billion and is now cash flow positive. With statistics like that, one would have a hard time suggesting that Airbnb is a 'failing company'. Looking solely at its booking growth rates, however, could suggest otherwise.

While booking rates is a real metric and is directly correlated to the success of the business, it can be misleading if taken out of context. The challenge with humans is that we all create our own version of the truth. The way you see a set of facts and figures may be different to how I would see them. We only have to look at the 'glass half full' analogy to understand the various ways that we can interpret facts differently.

In order to understand the real story, your numbers have to be presented in context. Looking at one metric exclusively runs the risk of making decisions based upon misleading information.

To counter this, you need to rely upon a balanced menu of indicators to understand what they are trying to tell you. Once you can understand what they mean, you can figure out how to most effectively tell that story to others.

Keystone Habits

As a sucker for 'self-help', productivity, and life-hack guides, I'm a big believer in experimenting with different habits and routines. Simple things like giving meditation a shot or having apple cider vinegar for breakfast. But there was one habit recommended to me which changed my life and business for the better. That habit was daily journaling.

Perched on my bedside table sits my journal, an old notebook that I scribble inside of every morning after waking up, and then again before going to bed.

What do I write? Nothing really. Just random thoughts, feelings, and emotions. What did I achieve? What could I do more of? Who did I meet? What am I grateful for? It gives me the space to ponder anything that's weighing on my mind.

It's an opportunity to unpack and reflect on the day.

A sacred, uninterrupted slice of time that is just mine.

The simple act of journaling has had a profound impact on my life. It helps me manifest my goals. It ignites my creativity. It helps me have greater focus and make better decisions. Daily journaling has been a catalyst which locks all my other habits into place. This is known as a keystone habit.

In his book, *The Power of Habit*, Charles Duhigg says that developing keystone habits is important for behavior change. He describes keystone habits as, "small changes or habits that people introduce into their routines that unintentionally carry over into other aspects of their lives."

For example, a person might start exercising once per week, and unknowingly begin to eat better and be more productive at work. Perhaps she begins to show more patience with her colleagues and loved ones. She may feel less stressed or anxious, and have increased motivation toward her goals. The ingrained patterns in her brain reform and she becomes an entirely different person. All because she started exercising once per week.

Keystone habits are powerful because they have ripple effects which can rapidly alter every aspect of your life. For your business, it's as simple as reviewing your finances regularly.

Reviewing your numbers on a regular basis is a keystone habit. Taking the time to objectively review your business from this lens can elevate you into a state of higher thinking. Use it as an opportunity to reflect on your financial performance. In this state, you will subconsciously be more aware of not overspending, weighing up risk and seeing how certain decisions will impact the other areas of your business.

Take my recipe book and implement it in your business. If you're new to reviewing your numbers frequently, start small.

You can begin by reviewing your monthly financials with your management team. If you're a solo founder, review them with an accountant or someone you trust.

Make the time to learn what the numbers are saying and how you can improve things. Take control of your machine and use your financial statements as a guide.

Which Numbers Do I Look At?

Communication with your customers is critical in business. Talking about your financial results with key stakeholders such as investors, management, and the rest of your staff is no different. You can't expect to empower your team to make decisions if they lack information or context.

They need tools to help you. Great staff will tell you what tools they need. But it's up to you to lead them.

The question you need to ask yourself always comes down to, what are the tools? What information do you share, and how much of it do you share?

In this chapter I'll help you build a powerful tool kit of numbers and reports that you can share with your stakeholders. To begin, ask yourself two questions: What's it for? and Who's it for?

What's It For?

If, just ten years ago, you asked James Watt "What is Brewdog for?" he'd probably talk about uniting the misfits, punks, and freaks under one banner to celebrate alternative thinking, character, and love of craft beer.

Today, the answer is clear. Backed by corporate private equity funds and investors, the purpose of Brewdog is to make as much money as possible. Everything else is in service of that goal.

Ask your typical CPA at a typical small business accounting firm what accounting is for and he'll probably say "it's to get your taxes done". Hopefully I've changed your mind about that.

My point is everything you do: every report, every piece of info has a purpose—ultimately, it's a story. The craft, then, is designing the story you want to tell, and thinking about who it's for.

Who's It For?

Your board of investors don't need to know that you are changing the coffee beans from medium to dark roast. Your caffeine-addicted operations manager might though. Once you've decided *what* the purpose of the report is for, you can then design *who* the information is for.

There are two groups of stakeholders in your business that need information to know if they are doing their job effectively:

1. Your Staff
2. Your Management Team / Board of Investors

YOUR STAFF

Your company-wide staff need to know how they are each contributing to the business. Without guidance, support, and measurable ways to gauge performance, they will be left in the dark.

So, what questions are they asking?

- How is the business going?
- Am I doing my work effectively?
- How does my daily work impact the business and its vision?
- What should we be doing differently?

All of the information that you share with your team should help them understand these core questions.

YOUR MANAGEMENT TEAM & BOARD OF INVESTORS

You could be a one-person CEO, or have a team of people in 'management positions' running various functions of your business. You could even have a board if you are large or have taken some form of investment. This category of stakeholders requires information to help drive strategic decisions.

What questions are they asking?

- What is the financial health of the business?
- Are we achieving our strategic and financial goals?
- What isn't working?
- What is working?

As you can see, different people will be asking different questions. It ultimately depends on their role in the business. This needs to be considered when presenting this information.

My Recipe Book of Numbers

I've done the hard part for you and outlined below a recipe book of financial numbers that you can share with each stakeholder. These numbers are applicable to both high-touch and low-touch business models, and they're just a start.

Some metrics may be relevant to your business, others less so. Accordingly, take time to think about the key performance drivers in your business, and how you can substitute them. As with everything feel free to experiment and add your own.

Okay, let's start with what to do on a weekly basis.

WEEKLY NUMBERS

The weekly numbers are operationally-focused. They are the leading indicators of your company's performance that you and your team own, influence, and drive. These include:

- Sales pipeline and expected sales for the week
- Employee Utilization Rate
- Number of outstanding customer support tickets
- Any critical customer feedback

Basically, any numbers that will be owned by your team.

I hate meetings. They are expensive and can be a waste of time if not everyone is onboard with the topic. If the purpose is for information gathering and sharing, it's important to have an agenda —and stick to it.

Go through these numbers with your team at the start of the week. My favorite time is 9 a.m. sharp, Monday morning. I like it because it gives your team enough time to settle in at the office after the weekend, to redirect their focus on what needs to be done.

The agenda for this meeting should be very simple and clear. It should be structured as follows:

- Review your previous week's results with the team
- Review the targets for the current week
- Discuss any key challenges or roadblocks

The purpose of this meeting is to set targets and focus your team. Accordingly, it should be no longer than an hour, tops. If you feel there is a big topic that's up for discussion, don't raise it in this meeting. Put it in a memo in advance for everyone to review, then setup a separate time to discuss it, if necessary.

MONTHLY NUMBERS – WITH MANAGEMENT & BOARD OF INVESTORS

The monthly numbers that you review are the bigger picture financials. These are the metrics that will give you and your management team a snapshot of your company's financial and overall performance.

A monthly management report should be generated by your finance team/accountant/bookkeeper, which covers the following key numbers:

- Profit & Loss actuals compared to budget
- Balance Sheet for current month, compared to last month
- Free Cash Flow
- Accounts Receivable Days

- Average Revenue per Customer
- Revenue per Employee
- Customer Churn Rate
- Customer Acquisition Costs
- Net Promoter Score
- Employee Turnover

Yes, I know it looks like a handful—but it's important. My recommendation is to stay on top of these numbers regularly. Remember that thing about good habits?

Your monthly management report should be issued and discussed with your team by the 15th of each month at the very latest. This gives enough time for your bookkeeper Sandra to get all the accounts reconciled up to date, but also so it isn't too late. It's hard to make decisions based on old information.

The agenda for this meeting will differ slightly, depending on the size of your management team, or whether you have a Board of Investors. At a core level, the agenda should look like this:

1. Discuss the numbers (as above)
2. Discuss any key strategic milestones and targets
3. Set actions for next month

MONTHLY NUMBERS – WITH YOUR WHOLE COMPANY

Early in my business I was afraid to share our company's financial results with our staff. I was afraid that if they saw the real financial picture, they might be concerned about our ability to pay their next paycheck.

This changed when one of our senior team members asked how the business was going, and if there was any way that they could help to improve sales.

My first reaction was "What the hell… That's what I pay you to do! You haven't been doing it all this time?"

I realized he simply lacked context. He doesn't know what I know, and I certainly don't know what he knows.

At our next monthly townhall, I ran an experiment. I decided to share the monthly financial results of our business. It was fair to say I was nervous. I had no idea what my staff would think about our financial position (and the state of it).

Turns out my team valued the transparency and started to suggest ways that we could improve our financial position—like how can we increase revenue per customer via upselling. They were interested in our performance and how their day-to-day activities tied back to the bigger picture.

Simply put, they were more engaged and started carrying a posture of a business owner. Their 'mini-business' is a part that they can control and own.

Empowering your staff to make decisions is a critical ingredient in scaling yourself from your machine. For people to make smart decisions, they need information and context around issues and their performance. Give it to them and don't be afraid to share.

You'll be surprised how a person's IQ jumps a few points as soon as she has the information and the authority to act. Your team also brings a different perspective of thinking, countering any biases that you have as a leader.

So, the question is, how much do you share?

In my business, we share the following information:

- Profit & Loss actuals compared to budget
- Accounts Receivable days
- Gross Profit Margin % trend line
- Average Revenue per Customer

It's important to not get too bogged down in the specifics. Showcasing the KPIs and numbers gives people a feel for how the company is performing, and helps them to understand how their daily activities impact those results.

Simply put, tell the story you want to tell. If you're trying to inspire your team because of low morale or performance, don't belabor every KPI. Talk about growth and the initiatives you're implementing to change things. In other words, use the numbers as a tool to drive the outcomes you want.

Sharing these numbers with your team will not only create a culture of transparency and accountability, it will also serve to educate and improve the financial literacy of your team members. We can all use a bit of that.

"I have no use for bodyguards, but I have very specific use for highly-trained certified public accountants."

Elvis Presley

HOW AN ACCOUNTANT ADDS VALUE TO YOUR BUSINESS

C'mon, I Can't Afford a CFO

Startup founders and small business owners often squirm at the idea of having a CFO in their business. I mean, I get it; the value of a CFO in a young company is a highly-contested subject.

So, do they add value?

We've talked about Bob the CPA a lot in the previous chapters. I'm positive you have a Bob that advises you and your business. I bet Bob helps you with your taxes and ensures you are compliant with the IRS. So, if every business already has a Bob, why do they need a CFO, too?

There is a worldview that CFOs are only for big business. They picture a grey-haired executive, managing balance sheets of billion-dollar corporations. They drive shiny Porches, demand whopping salaries, and speak in tongues (aka corporate jargon).

While this may be the case with traditional CFOs, a commercially-minded and savvy financial accountant can add an enormous amount of value to your growing business. They can provide tactical and strategic advice to help you improve cash flow, forecast financial performance, and give you visibility over the levers you can pull in your business to improve profitability.

Basically, a solid financial accountant adds steroids to the core Principles that I've shared within this book.

This Person Doesn't Exist for Small Businesses

Despite the value a financial accountant can add, it's my experience that the need for strategic information is largely unmet for small companies. Many founders assume Bob the CPA will give them this advice. Unfortunately, this isn't always the case. Of course, there are outliers, but the large majority of tax accountants don't deliver on these services.

Why? Because Bob is too busy servicing your tax needs. He will tell you what you can or can't claim. He will help you with structuring so that you have your assets protected. He will ensure you remain compliant with the IRS.

Don't get me wrong—maintaining compliance with regulatory bodies is very important. My point is, there is a difference between a commercial-minded financial manager/CFO and your CPA Bob. Technically, they're both CPAs.

Your tax accountant's focus is on reducing your taxes. A financial manager's focus is about driving financial performance.

These are completely different perspectives.

So, What Does a Small Business Need?

The dilemma is that while every business can derive value from a CFO's financial capability—it comes at a price. The dilemma is this: Does the value that a CFO creates outweigh the cost?

In this chapter, you will learn what you should be getting from your accountant based on your phase of business growth. But first, allow me to explain the functions that an accountant performs.

On the next page, I made another little napkin sketch. This one outlines the hierarchy of financial needs for any kind of business.

I separated these needs into the various functions that an owner should be concerned about. Let's look at them one-by-one:

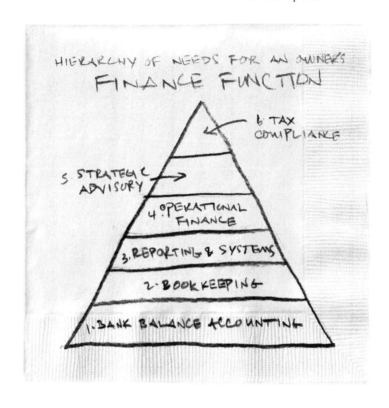

LEVEL 1 – BANK BALANCE ACCOUNTING

Bank balance accounting is the most primitive and basic form of accounting. Typically conducted in spreadsheets, you tally all your expenses and income from your bank statements for the sole purpose of filing your tax. The advantages of this form of record keeping is that it's cheap and easy to do. It's a popular method for solopreneurs and businesses just getting started.

My recommendation is that you can get away with this form of record keeping up to around $250k of annualized revenue. Once your business grows past that, it's time to upgrade.

LEVEL 2 – ACCURAL BASED BOOKKEEPING

Accruals-based bookkeeping adds extra punch to bank balance accounting and sets the foundation to your finance function. It's the process of taking the building blocks of financial data and structuring them into a format for interpretation and analysis.

Most business owners view bookkeeping as a compliance-driven activity. It is often perceived as a low-value, commoditized administrative function. This is a deadly misconception.

The reality is that bookkeeping is the most valuable layer of your business as it underpins the finance function of your entire organization.

There comes a time where every business owner should outsource their bookkeeping to a professional service provider. I recommend you should do this as early as commercially possible, so your bookkeeper can learn the ins and outs of your business— before you scale or grow quickly. Remember, your precious time should be spent on high leverage activities. Delegate and outsource anything that isn't high leverage.

Bookkeeping should be maintained at least on a weekly basis, with the target of closing month-end within 14 days. This allows appropriate time to measure your results and make decisions from the numbers (see Level 3 below).

LEVEL 3 – REPORTING AND SYSTEMS

With your data and transactions being correctly accounted for, the next step is to report on the activity of your business. With so much financial data generated in your business, it's easy to get overwhelmed with the amount of information. Simplicity is the key. A good financial manager will work with you to establish additional systems to monitor and measure the information.

This business data is not exclusive to your finances either. You want to be measuring and managing other aspects of your business like operations, sales and marketing, and people.

The primary purpose of reporting is to communicate this business information to your relevant stakeholders. Accordingly, it's all about context. As I said before, what you report to your management team will be different to what is reported to your Board of Investors. A financial manager will help you identify your 'Who's it for?' and establish a system from there.

LEVEL 4 – OPERATIONAL FINANCE

Operational finance is the process of taking your historical data and using it to build forecasts and predictive reporting. It's the process of developing a rolling budget, maintaining short-range cash flow forecasts, and undertaking analysis on your target financial performance compared to your actual activity. For start-ups, this is critical, so you're on top of your burn rate and runway.

Operational finance can go hand-in-hand with reporting by a commercially-minded financial manager. It's common for a CFO to have input into this function as well.

LEVEL 5 – STRATEGIC ADVISORY

Strategic advisory is the sweet spot of a CFO. Partnering with a strategic CFO can help you build the financial and operational strategy of your business. She can help you deal with funding mechanisms, pricing, capital raising, mergers and acquisitions, and long-term shareholder creation. If you aim to be a 'big' business, a strategic CFO is worth their weight in gold.

LEVEL 6 – TAX COMPLIANCE

Tax is at the top of the needs pyramid because every business needs to file their taxes. Ensure you work with a tax accountant that knows your industry and business model so you are operating from the right structure and maximizing all of the tax incentives and deductions available to you.

The Minimum Viable Finance Function

So, what services do you need when building out the accounting capability of your business?

Based on my experience in the industry and working with clients, here's a guide of what it should it look like.

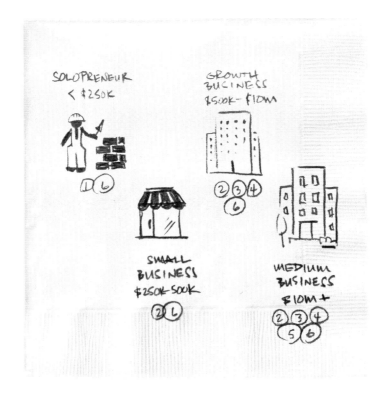

Of course, your specific requirements may differ, depending on your type of business.

For example, if you have external investors, despite your revenue and size, they will want regular updates on the financial position of your company, so it warrants an operational finance capability.

Should I Outsource or In-Source this Function?

A common question I'm asked is whether you should outsource or directly employ your finance team.

Refer back to Chapter 20 where I spoke about outsourcing and your business's core competencies. As a refresher, your priority as a founder is to focus on the competencies of your business. In other words, you should only directly employ staff that are attributable to growing those competencies, and growing revenue.

Doing accounting and bookkeeping is not a core competency if you sell baby formula like Sarah, or sell advertising like Brendan. It is not a good use of your time either.

So, the answer is outsource it.

When it comes to finance, technology has lowered the barriers to entry for highly-capable and experienced financial managers and CFOs that offer their services at a fraction of the rate of a full-time employee. Typically, these accountants are called either financial managers and virtual CFOs.

What to Look For in a Finance Team

When looking to engage with service providers to manage your finance function, ask yourself these questions:

1. DO THEY HAVE EXPERIENCE IN MY INDUSTRY?

It's critically important that your advisors have an intimate understanding of your business model and industry. This ensures you're leveraging their industry experience and knowledge relevant to your company.

2. DO THEY HAVE THE CAPABILITY TO GROW WITH ME?

If you're a high-growth business, ensure that your providers can grow with you—especially in resource-intensive roles like bookkeeping. Ensure that you partner with a bookkeeper and financial manager that can scale up with your organization. This means you will not have to continually replace and retrain people as you grow.

3. DO I TRUST THEM?

Working with a great finance partner is like a marriage. They will be backing you and won't be afraid to have hard conversations. Rapport is therefore important. Ask yourself, do I like this team and can I work with them?

In summary, working with a good financial manager can add a lot of value to helping you achieve your business goals. Knowing how to design it is half the battle.

Principle 5 Takeaways

- Paying attention to your One Thing can give you the focus to drive your company's financial and overall performance. The key here is to keep it simple.

- Recipe Book for Numbers

    ° Every week, report everything on an operational level
    ° Every month, report everything at a financial level

- Don't be afraid to share your financials with your team members. They need information and context to do their job. Inform and empower them.

- You probably don't need a CFO in your business... yet. What you need is a financial manager. If you're not getting this level of service from Bob the CPA, find someone else.

- When engaging a financial manager, ensure that:

    ° They have experience in your industry
    ° They have the capability to grow with you
    ° You trust them!

Conclusion

NAKED AS A WAY OF LIFE

NUMBERS REVEAL THE TRUTH

Like many entrepreneurs, I dressed my financials in fancy clothes. But no more. Now my numbers are stark naked. I see them for what they really are. It's time to get to work!

"Why does man not see things? He is himself in the way: he conceals things."

Friedrich Nietzsche

STARK NAKED CONCLUSION

How to Uncover a New Friend

Elon Musk famously quipped that "being an entrepreneur is like chewing glass and staring into the abyss". I've never tried eating glass, but I get the point. Business can be brutal.

In your business journey you will inevitably run into moments where you think the world is crumbling around you. Like my 'freakout' moment I described in the first chapter—I thought everything had imploded. I wanted to throw it all in. Irrational fear paralyzed me. It constricted my ability to make good decisions.

Ever tried to make a long-term decision while drowning?

Perhaps there are moments when you respond to challenges with aggression. Or times when you dress yourself up in layers of bravado to fight the good fight. We all need a bit of the Steve Jobs effect. But we also need to ensure that our 'reality distortion field' doesn't inundate our ability to make smart decisions.

Whatever posture you decide is best to carry on that day, one thing that doesn't change is your need to see the truth. You can't understand the root cause of the problems in your business if the facts are clouded with your bias.

Your numbers can help you to see things for what they really are. The truth they reveal is, ultimately, your friend.

You just need to uncover them.

You need to see them stark naked.

Accounting is Accountability

Accounting is not about your taxes. It's not about GAAP or ratios or metrics. It's not about old dudes in tweed suits with calculators.

No. Accounting is accountability. Used in the right way, it can help you to achieve your goals, to march towards your mission, and to build your legacy.

I've experienced firsthand how numbers have helped me to grow and build a sustainable, vital business.

My sincere hope is that you can use it in the same way I do.

Frequently Asked Financial Questions

Throughout this book I've shared a number of principles and tactics to help you navigate the many financial landmines that your company will inevitably face.

No matter the phase of your venture—whether you're in startup or scale-up—shit will happen. Things will go wrong. I guarantee it. What underpins your success is how you respond.

We've followed the journey of Brendan and Sarah throughout the book to demonstrate these principles in a practical setting. I want to conclude their stories by returning to a few core questions. Questions that my clients, all founders like yourself, ask me daily.

FAQ 1 – WHEN CAN I AFFORD TO HIRE MY NEXT EMPLOYEE?

When it comes to growth, it's natural for us to assume that hiring more people is the solution to achieve your business goals. Employees can add a great deal of value. But they also come with a lot of costs—both financial and mental.

Before assuming you need to hire more staff, ask yourself: Do I need to? Or, better yet, can I?

When reviewing business functions you want to remove from your to-do list, consider the framework:

- Eliminate
- Automate
- Outsource

Once you've decided that you need to hire more staff, remember the 2x New Revenue Rule. That is:

- Have forecasted sales of at least 2x the monthly salary; and
- Always have 2x months of wages as cash in the bank

Following this rule of thumb will ensure that your business can support the additional financial and time costs of your new hires. In other words, you can grow profitably—not 'into the red'.

FAQ 2 – HOW CAN I INCREASE MY PROFIT?

When it comes to increasing your profit, don't assume that cost cutting is the best answer. The three Profit Levers we discussed in the book are not created equal. Here's their ranking by effectiveness:

- Sales Lever (increase prices)
- Direct Costs (decrease costs)
- Operations Costs (decrease costs)
- Sales Lever (increase volume)

Remember also the profit-improving tactics we covered. For high-touch business models, the top three are:

- **Cull Your Customers**
  It's likely that the top 20% of your customers are absorbing the losses of your bottom 80%. You need to continually perform a profitability analysis on each one (Chapter 10).

- **Clone Your Best Customers**
  A profitability analysis will not only illuminate your worst customers, it'll identify your best ones. Figure out how you can 'clone' your best customers—that is, find more like them.

- **Optimize Your Productivity**
  In high-touch businesses, your employees are your product. They are also your largest asset. The key is to ensure that you leverage their time and abilities so they can be effective.

If you have a low-touch businees model, we talked about a few profit-improving tactics as well. The three best ones are:

- **Know Your Product Mix**
  Your product mix is the dark art of blending marketing and finance. It's understanding how to maximize the overall gross profit of your company by tinkering with the product mix.

- **Increase Sales Volume**
  Try to make incremental improvements to your sales funnel. Big changes start with small steps.

- **Optimize Your Customer Acquisition Costs**
  If you don't, you run the risk of spending too much money to acquire those new customers—more than they are worth.

FAQ 3 — WHERE IS MY CASH?

Your cash is hiding in your balance sheet. More specifically, your 'working capital'. Your working capital is all your short term assets and liabilities like your accounts receivable, inventory, and accounts payable.

I hope by this point I've emphasized how important it is to have actual cash, the free and fluid kind, sitting in your account.

FAQ 4 – HOW DO I IMPROVE MY CASH FLOW?

Focus on reducing your cash conversion cycle. This measure the amount of time (in days) it takes to convert your profits into cash.

You can knock some time off of your company's cycle by:

- Reducing accounts receivable days
- Reducing inventory days
- Increasing accounts payable days.

Cash flow is all about effective working capital management. Run experiments and focus on getting it as low as possible.

FAQ 5 – HOW DO I CALCULATE MY CHARGE-OUT RATE?

The best businesses price the customer. In other words, price on value—not time taken to complete a project. However, if you're cornered into a situation where time-based billing is a necessity, it's helpful to have a base charge out rate to ensure you are not discounting your value.

Charge-out rates are built on three crucial components:

- Your firm's revenue per employee target
- Total number of working hours per annum
- Target 'utilization' rate

Refer to Chapter 19 for this calculation.

FAQ 6 – WHICH NUMBERS SHOULD I BE LOOKING AT?

Assessing your numbers on a regular basis is a keystone habit. Taking the time to objectively review your business can help you reflect on your financial performance. You will subconsciously be more aware of not overspending, weighing up risk, and seeing how decisions will impact other areas of your business.

The numbers you should be regularly reviewing are as follows:

WEEKLY NUMBERS (OPERATIONALLY FOCUSED)

- Sales pipeline and expected sales for the week
- Employee Utilization Rate
- Number of outstanding customer support tickets
- Any critical customer feedback

MONTHLY NUMBERS (FINANCIAL HEALTH)

- Profit & Loss actuals compared to budget
- Balance Sheet for current month, compared to last month
- Free Cash Flow
- Accounts Receivable Days
- Average Revenue per Customer
- Revenue per Employee
- Customer Churn Rate
- Customer Acquisition Costs
- Net Promoter Score
- Employee Turnover

Sharing these numbers with your team can create a culture of transparency and accountability. It also serves to educate everyone inside the company, and improve their financial literacy.

I suggest sharing your monthly numbers with your investors, as well. Remember, they too are owners of your company and they have the right to be informed about how their investment is going.

FAQ 7 – HOW MUCH CAN I SPEND ON CUSTOMER ACQUISITION?

Start by understanding the lifetime value of your customers, or Customer Lifetime Value. This dictates how much you can afford to spend on marketing to profitably acquire them in the first place.

A great rule of thumb is that the ratio of your customer lifetime value to acquisition cost should be equal to or greater than 3:1.

In other words, for every dollar you spend on acquiring a customer, that customer should be worth at least three times that value to your company.

FAQ 8 – HOW DO I CALCULATE MY BURN RATE AND RUNWAY?

Your company's burn rate is not the same as the losses per your P&L. Your burn rate is negative Free Cash Flow.

You can calculate your burn rate by taking your current month's burn rate and dividing it by the amount of cash in the bank.

FAQ 9 – AS A FOUNDER, HOW MUCH SHOULD I PAY MYSELF?

The art is finding a balance that gives you enough income to support the lifestyle you need, while still providing the business with the funds it needs to fuel healthy growth.

You can do the former by understanding your Minimum Viable Lifestyle.

Decisionem

Latin for the word 'decision' literally means 'to cut off'. How I interpret this is that decision-making is not about making choices, but rather about 'cutting-off' choices.

Eliminating choices until you are left with one.

To you that may sound limiting, even suffocating. But to me, it's not. It's liberating.

Having many choices and keeping our options open is good. But, if we're serious about where we want to go, serious about achieving what we desire, then we need to make choices—choices that often have trade-offs.

Numbers can help you separate the signals from the noise. They can guide you to the path of attaining what you really want.

Fundamentally, numbers uncover the truth. You need to reveal them in their stark naked glory, to see them for what they are.

Now get to work!

AUTHOR BIO

Jason Andrew is a Chartered Accountant, investor, and founder of Arbor Group, a technology-first financial services company serving entrepreneurs globally.

With over a decade of experience as a business and corporate advisor, Jason advises on a range of areas including mergers and acquisitions, transaction services, financial strategy and performance improvement.

Jason is passionate about helping business owners extract value from their numbers and data. His personal mission is to improve the financial literacy of entrepreneurs and change the current worldview of the accounting profession.

Jason writes long-form content on finance and decision making for business owners. His work has been featured in *Business Insider*, Intuit Global, and Xero. Jason was recently announced as one of Smart Company's Top 20 Business Thinkers for 2018.

Jason currently resides in Brisbane, Australia, with his wife Liz and doggo Bella.

Printed in Poland
by Amazon Fulfillment
Poland Sp. z o.o., Wrocław

26813984R00159